Watchmen in the Night

Previous books by Theodore C. Sorensen

Decision-making in the White House (1963)
Kennedy (1965)
The Kennedy Legacy (1969)

Watchmen in the Night
Presidential Accountability after Watergate

Theodore C. Sorensen

The MIT Press
Cambridge, Massachusetts, and London, England

This book was set in CRT Baskerville,
printed on R&E Book,
and bound in Columbia MBV-4492
by The Colonial Press Inc.
in the United States of America

Library of Congress Cataloging in Publication Data

Sorensen, Theodore C
  Watchmen in the night.

  Bibliography: p.
  Includes index.
  1. Executive power—United States. 2. Separation of powers—United States. 3. Watergate Affair, 1972–
  I. Title.
  JK516.S67   353.03′2   75-1273
  ISBN 0-262-19133-4

To Gillian

Contents

Foreword   xi

Preface   xv

I The Past as Prologue

1 Was Watergate a Deterrent?   3

2 Was Nixon an Aberrant?   13

II The Illusion of Omnipotence

3 The Facade of Unlimited Presidential Power   27

  Inherent Limitations   29

  Institutional Limitations   33

    The Departments and Career Service   33

    The Press   37

    Congress   41

    The Courts   47

4 The Myth of the Strong Nixon Presidency   53

5 The Legacy of the Weak Nixon Presidency   63

  The Effect of the Nixon Ouster   65

  The Danger of an Impotent Presidency   70

  Proposed Structural Changes   76

III The Sinews of Accountability

6 Making the President More Accountable to Congress   85

  Confirming the Cabinet   91

Pruning White House Staff Functions   97
Securing Information   102
Overseeing Surveillance   109
Withdrawing Emergency Powers   113

7 Making the President More Accountable to the Courts 117
The President in Court   118
Congress in Court   132
The Department of Justice in Court   134

8 Making the President More Accountable to the People 139
The Mystique of the President   139
The Media and the President   144
The Marketing of the President   146
The Measuring of the President   151

Sources and Notes   161

Acknowledgments   169

Index   171

This nation . . . has no right to expect that it will always have wise and humane rulers, sincerely attached to the principles of the Constitution. Wicked men, ambitious of power, with hatred of liberty and contempt of law, may fill the place once occupied by Washington and Lincoln . . . .

United States Supreme Court
Ex Parte Milligan
71 U.S. (4 Wallace) 2, 125 (1866)

Foreword

During Franklin Roosevelt's "hundred days" politicians tumbled over one another in rushing to support him. "I will do anything you ask," an Iowa congressman wrote the President. "You are my leader." Later, when the economic crisis had subsided, many of the same people were calling FDR a dictator. He was accused of seeking "one-man power" when he ran for a third term; he was hailed as an inspired leader in the months after Pearl Harbor; he was called an oppressor during the days of rationing and price control. Harry Truman and Lyndon Johnson experienced comparable changes of image.

Stupendous pressures at home and abroad will bear down on President Ford during the last two years of Richard Nixon's vacated term. If history repeats itself, these pressures will be accompanied by stentorian calls for presidential leadership, even presidential dictatorship. If Mr. Ford finds it impossible to assume the role of heroic leadership, he will be succeeded in 1976 by a Democrat or a Republican who, like FDR, will offer "action—and action now!" And that man too will be applauded, only to be castigated later for his assumption of dictatorial power.

Not only does the pendulum swing between the actual exercise of greater and lesser presidential power. A pendulum oscillates even more sharply between a public opinion first calling for, and then repudiating, the heroic type of leader. We build our triumphal arches out of bricks, Mr. Dooley observed, so we will have missiles handy to topple our heroes. If the two pendulums parallel one another, however, one is always behind the other. Public opinion reacts to the latest crisis of governmental inactivity or overactivity rather than trying to anticipate and plan for firm and steady leadership in future crises.

Is there any way out of the trap of pendulum thinking? If we address the problem of controlling power with the clear and steady vision of the framers of the Constitution, we would understand that the cardinal problem is not the amount of power but the control and accountability of power. "In framing a government which is to be administered by men over men," wrote the author of Federalist 51,". . . you must first enable the government to control the governed; and in the next place oblige it to control itself." And this was to be done "by so contriving the interior structure of the government as that its several constituent parts may, by their mutual relations, be the means of keeping each other in their proper places." Ambition must be made to counteract ambition. Because they understood both the springs of human action and the contrivances of government, the framers wrote the Constitution that during most of its life has made it possible to check and balance executive, legislative, and judicial power.

The cardinal aim, in short, was not to destroy power but to make it accountable. And accountability, in the broadest sense of responsibility to Congress, to the courts, to the public, and ultimately to "history," is the yardstick that Theodore Sorensen brings to the question of the balanced exercise of presidential power. This is an old American problem on which

Mr. Sorensen throws shafts of new light. He understands that power cannot be ignored or exorcised or banished; it must be identified and confronted. In his propositions that Nixon was not a strong but a desperately weak President; that presidential improvisation can easily slide over into presidential usurpation of power; that—as shown in some of the author's most trenchant pages—the power of the President to "go to the country" or to appeal to the reporters (or to their bosses) is sharply limited; that we cannot contain the presidential demon by eviscerating it (for example, by separating out ceremonial from political powers), he has challenged some of the assumptions of both the upholders and dethroners of presidential power.

This study, in short, is a very fresh treatment of a very old institution. Mr. Sorensen's achievement is due in large measure, I would judge, to his experience within the White House, to his own opportunity to feel and touch and taste and smell the Presidency from inside as well as to the later detachment that enabled him to see the origins of some of the misdeeds of "bad" Presidents in the enthusiastically applauded earlier acts of "good" Presidents. In appraising the institution with such familiarity and with steady and unclouded insight, in distinguishing between the real and spurious dangers of the strong Presidency, and in thus helping prevent the pendulum of presidential power from taking further wild oscillations, the author himself joins the small band of informed, vigilant, and farsighted Presidency-scrutinizers who can take their places among the watchmen in the night.

James MacGregor Burns

Preface

This is not another history of the Presidency. Arthur Schlesinger in *The Imperial Presidency* has brilliantly traced the evolution of the war-making and other powers of that office. Emmet Hughes in *The Living Presidency* has thoughtfully examined its place in our history and system. I could not hope to add to these excellent recent works.

Nor is this another book about what happened at Watergate. Like millions of others, I was both fascinated and horrified by the evidence of massive corruption and criminality in the White House. But also like them, I have only the knowledge of those events that could be learned through the news media. The inside story I gladly leave to the participants. Some of them will have ample time on their hands to write about it.

Nor, finally, is this book a plea to restore or remember Camelot. On the contrary, Camelot-like glorifications of the Presidency are part of the problem. Despite some notorious mistakes—including the Bay of Pigs, fallout shelters, the missile gap, and Vietnam—the Kennedy Administration, with its high ideals and spirited approach, unintentionally raised public expectations of the Presidency to a level that facilitated subsequent attempts to monopolize power in the White House. In truth there never was a Camelot—only an honest, hardworking Administration, as prone to error as any other collection of humans. True, it was light years away from the

Nixon era in the myriad of ways discussed herein; but the clock cannot and should not ever be turned back.

This small volume is intended instead to examine from the viewpoint of a lawyer who knows the office from the inside what effect Watergate might have and should have on the future of the American Presidency. It was prompted by the kind invitation of The Massachusetts Institute of Technology and The MIT Press to deliver a series of lectures on this topic in the fall of 1974 on which such a book might be based.

I accepted their invitation because of my deep concern over two conflicting but pervasive public reactions to Watergate regarding the Presidency—an underreaction, which assumed that the departure of Richard Nixon left no further problem; and an overreaction, which called for emasculating the office to "prevent another Nixon."

Both were shortsighted reactions to immediate events that failed to take into account a longer view. I understand this error, having committed it myself a decade ago.

Having served in the White House and written two books on the subject, I thought I knew a fair amount about the uses of presidential power. I didn't know half as much as I thought I did. I knew a fair amount about one President. I knew something about the Presidency. But John F. Kennedy's two immediate successors operated the same levers of government so differently than he did, and utilized the same powers of that position for purposes and in a manner so unlike his own, that it gradually became clear to me that many of my generalizations about the good that would flow from every aggrandizement of that office were more hope than reality.

Even though in my previous books I had acknowledged necessary limitations on presidential authority, I had regarded the Presidency in ideal terms, as had the President for whom I worked. I had valued its powers in the belief that they were indispensable tools for waging peace, not war, expanding human rights, not invading them, and spurring respect for the law, not violations. I helped write John Kennedy's speeches on a strong Presidency, and helped him forge the legal tools of a stronger Presidency, in the mistaken belief that what was good for the Presidency would inevitably be good for the country.

Yet I have not joined, and indeed have found profoundly disturbing, the recent sudden conversion of many American liberals to a preference for a weak Presidency—after supporting a strong Presidency as long as the office was occupied by a liberal committed to the policies they favored. Nevertheless, I have come to recognize the imbalance in my previous views and to see that it is possible for the emperor to have no clothes.

Whatever the illusions of the past, no thoughtful American favors today either an all-powerful President or a weak figurehead President. The question is what needs changing and how. When we were all "wallowing" in Watergate, too much was happening to afford much time to think about its implications for the future. Yet it raised questions more fundamental to our system than any raised since the Constitutional Convention, with the possible exception of those preceding the Civil War.

Now, between Watergate and our national bicentennial, is an appropriate time for a new national debate on the powers of the Presidency. The time available for the preparation of the lectures on which this book is based was too limited to permit the necessary exposition, illustration, or documentation of all points; but it is my hope that this volume will nevertheless make some small contribution to that debate. Its basic thesis is that we must make certain changes which take Watergate and other recent events into account without letting them distort our long-range perspective—that our nation will continue to need great power in the Presidency, but that we must do more to hold it accountable.

I

The Past as Prologue

1
Was Watergate a Deterrent?

To my surprise, a sense of sadness overtook my sense of relief when I heard the Thirty-seventh President of the United States announce that he would be the first to resign that office. Yet throughout the country the forced departure of Richard Nixon was greeted with pleasure and even exultation. Across from the White House, young celebrants snake-danced through Lafayette Park. Whatever the problem was, implied the national reaction, it was solved. The system had worked; the people reigned supreme. "Our long national nightmare is over," proclaimed the new President the next day. "Our Constitution works. Our great republic is a government of laws and not of men."

A surfeit of self-congratulation swept the United States. Columnists who weeks earlier had feared for the future of the nation now proclaimed that our governmental and political institutions had been strengthened. Historians who had previously termed Watergate a shocking demonstration of our system's inadequacies now called it proof of its resilience. The *New York Times* concluded that "the long and unmistakable drift toward concentration of power in the hands of one elected official, the President of the United States, has been stopped." Members of Congress proudly assured themselves that their rightful role in the constitutional balance had been restored.

Without Nixon to kick around any more, the country seemed finally prepared to heed his earlier urging that we "put Watergate behind us." No President hereafter, it was reasoned, would dare attempt a similar grab for power. "Wildly improbable," wrote the distinguished historian Henry Steele Commager. "There is little danger," wrote one of our most thoughtful observers, James Reston, "that we will have another White House gang like this one." Not for at least 50 years, ran the 1873–1923–1973–2023 cyclical theory advanced—with only part of his tongue in cheek—by Arthur Schlesinger in *The Imperial Presidency*.

The evils of the imperial Presidency itself were all but forgotten. Had not the new President pledged openness, accessibility, and a more important role for Congress and Cabinet members? He had indeed—but so had Richard Nixon upon taking office. Had not the new President in discussing the deplorable state of the economy been refreshingly frank? He had indeed—but every new President is frank about the economic problems he inherits from his predecessor.

Had not the new President, toasting his own English muffins and invoking the Golden Rule, inspired the country with his humble simplicity and bluntness? He had indeed—but a fortnight earlier, before that mantle of presidential mystique descended upon him, causing everyone to regard him with awe, those very same traits (differently labeled) had aroused scorn and disdain. We were witnessing in those first weeks after the Ford inauguration, Joe McGinniss wrote, "The Selling of the President 1974 . . . This time we, the people, are not only the consumers but the merchandisers as well . . . creating an idol whom, history suggests, we will eventually feel compelled to destroy."

One month later, some who had rejoiced the most about the marvelous change in White House methods of operation were the most apoplectic about President Ford's one-man, secretly evolved, surprise decision to pardon his predecessor from all federal crimes committed as President. "[G]ood old open-Presidency Gerald R. Ford," wrote historian Barbara Tuchman, "had . . . hardly . . . settled in the ambience of the White House than he began to talk like Louis XIV and behave like Richard M. Nixon."

The high hopes of August 1974 were understandable. A new beginning is always a season for hope, and we did have reason for pride. Those who said that the Ford pardon of Nixon justified total cynicism and distrust in the system exaggerated as much then as they had a month earlier in proclaiming that all was well. After all, our nation's most powerful leader, reelected with a record majority in November 1972, had been forced to resign his office in August 1974 through the work of Congress, the courts, the Constitution, and an uncowed free press. Illicit pursuits at the highest levels of government had been detected and turned back, and nearly all of the participants turned out of government and in most instances brought to justice.

Our system had survived with honor a series of constitutional crises more serious than any since the Civil War. Unprecedented crises. The President had rejected several congressional subpoenas; fired the first Special Prosecutor; insisted that the second had no right to subpoena evidence from him; been named by a federal grand jury as an unindicted co-conspirator; considered rejecting a Supreme

Court order to turn over tapes; vowed not to resign his office so long as one Senator opposed his conviction on impeachable offenses; and displayed behavior sufficiently erratic to cause the Secretary of Defense and others to stay close to their offices lest a real or manufactured nuclear confrontation or some other improper command to the military be ordered.

Each of those crises was filled with explosive danger. But in the end the rule of law and the will of the people were peacefully upheld. Without either mobs or tanks in the streets, the government changed hands. To that extent our system did work and worked well. No pardon can take that away. There was indeed reason for pride.

But there was hardly grounds for euphoria. Despite its ultimate outcome, which did demonstrate some basic strengths in our institutions, Watergate also revealed their frightening vulnerability. We came painfully, dangerously close to a successful alteration of our form of government by stealth— painfully, dangerously close to a successful corruption of our political process, a usurpation of our basic rights of liberty and privacy, a subversion of our democratic institutions and constitutional balance, and a gross misuse of governmental power and agencies.

It was only sheer, hairbreadth chance that these particular conspirators at every level and every stage lacked skill as well as scruples. What if the cover-up of the original cover-up's cover-up had succeeded, or at least had not been taped? What if the Watergate burglars had not been such bunglers? Indeed, what if there had been no Watergate break-in at all?

Inasmuch as that act was no more essential to Nixon's

reelection than his illegal corporate campaign contributions, he would in all likelihood still be President today. A subversion of our system more serious than the break-in would now be continuing unabated. By now we would be into Phase II, previewed by Nixon's muttered threat on the tape of September 15, 1972, with regard to his detractors:

They are asking for it and they are going to get it. We have not used the power . . . the [Federal] Bureau [of Investigation] . . . the Justice Department. But things are going to change now.

Things have changed, although not quite in the way he envisioned. Removing the perpetrators of Watergate, even without altering the environment in which they operated, should teach some future White House occupants the necessity of not trying something similar. But it may only teach others the necessity of not being caught. History has never proven to be a very strong deterrent. The uproar over mink coats in the Truman White House did not prevent an uproar over vicuna coats in the Eisenhower White House. A Congress zealous enough to cause the impeachment of Andrew Johnson did not instill any fear of discovery and retribution in the miscreants who served under Ulysses Grant. Both Andrew Johnson's accusers and his defenders predicted after the fiasco of his impeachment and acquittal that Congress would "never again" undertake to impeach a President—but they were wrong.

Next time there may be no telltale adhesive tape left on a Watergate hall door or telltale magnetic tapes silently recording the cover-up, no Woodward and Bernstein to persist for the press, no Judge John Sirica to threaten (with questionable fairness) provisional or indeterminate sentences from the bench. Next time, the improved technology of surveillance, communications, and firepower which has made freedom so much more vulnerable elsewhere in the world may be used successfully against freedom in our own country.

"Watergate"—in the collective sense in which it will be used throughout this book to refer to all the assorted acts of presidential usurpation or abuse of power which were considered by the House Judiciary Committee impeachment proceeding—began long before the actual break-in. Still another twenty-six long and damaging months passed between the break-in and Nixon's final exposure and resignation. The delay, the damage endured, and above all the danger that it might well have been worse, should give us pause before we dismiss the possibility of future threats. Our nation has been well-served by Frank Wills, the forgotten watchman in the Watergate building. But how well has it been served by our national watchmen—the press, Congress, the bureaucracies, the judiciary, and the public?

The press was instrumental in exposing this sordid chapter in our history. But, except for the *Washington Post*, the press—despite its antipathy to Nixon—was initially slow to dig for the real facts. Even later, the bulk of the investigative effort was carried by a comparative few. Most newspapers are not prepared to conduct independent investigations of the President. Television and radio stations, licensed by the federal government, generally offer skimpy if sometimes jolly Washington news coverage. Except as used by a few aggressive reporters like Dan Rather, the enormous resources of network-broadcast news uncovered almost none of the major Watergate leads. The weekly news magazines, consistently superb on Watergate once it was rolling, obviously cannot hold the President accountable daily.

Congress, particularly through the Special Committee of the Senate headed by Sam Ervin and the Judiciary Committee of the House headed by Peter Rodino, played an effective role in exposing the facts of Watergate. But that was only after the members of Congress had blocked at least one earlier committee investigation; rejected even token cuts in appropriations for a White House staff that treated them with unconcealed contempt; renewed the President's discretionary White House fund even when he refused to tell them how it was spent; encouraged presidential disregard for the Constitution by accepting an erosion of their powers over war, treaties, and the nation's purse strings; and continued to delegate still new powers and functions to a President who, in the opinion of many, was already showing signs of megalomania.

Unwilling for too many years either to reduce its own penchant for secrecy or to enact effective campaign finance reforms, a Congress not unaccustomed to ethical slippage in Washington might well have tolerated—or at least not successfully challenged—most of the Watergate misdeeds, had not so many flagrant violations of law been automatically recorded on tapes which were surprisingly preserved, expletives undeleted, for all to hear.

Some bureau chiefs and career civil servants in the FBI,

CIA, Department of Justice, and Internal Revenue Service helped stop the spread of Watergate by ultimately saying "no" to the White House. But enough of them earlier said "yes" to cast doubt upon the reliability of the professional bureaucracy as an adequate future safeguard against presidential abuse.

Nor can the federal judiciary act as a sufficient bulwark, despite the indispensable contribution to Watergate justice made by Judges Sirica, Gessell, and others, ultimately including a unanimous Supreme Court. The judicial branch can and did check crimes brought to its attention after the fact. But it did nothing, and can in the future do nothing, about impropriety, falsehood, incompetence, or irrationality exercised in a President's office or within his campaign committee.

Finally, how much reassurance for the future can we find in the American public's role in the resolution of Watergate? Wise old Gunnar Myrdal said this episode brought out our highest ideals, and I would like to think he was right. But the number of prayers suddenly voiced on the jailhouse steps by the reverend Charles Colson and others is hardly proof of a national renaissance of public ethics and morality. Virtually all of the less desirable Nixon traits, which prominent Republicans and others began to deplore so openly upon his fall from grace, were public knowledge for years. But he did not seize or steal the 1972 election. Forty-nine of the fifty states handed it over to him.

Even after the scope of the scandal became clear, large segments of the public—at first aroused—became bored with new Watergate exposés. Immunity to shock rose with each incredible revelation. Some people found it too complex to follow, or dismissed it as an invention of the establishment press, or shrugged it off with the assertion that "everyone does it." To the very end, some refused to believe that their President could do wrong. Even after Nixon's resignation, 22 percent of those polled by Gallup in a special survey for *Newsweek* believed "his actions regarding Watergate were not serious enough to warrant his resignation;" and 33 percent believed "Nixon's political enemies unfairly exaggerated his actions in order to force him out of office." [1]

No doubt completion of the total impeachment and conviction process by the House and Senate, or even a comprehensive report complete with accurate tape transcripts, would have helped open the eyes of some of these loyalists, and, more importantly, helped those trying to formulate more precise standards of presidential conduct for the future. No doubt completion of the criminal justice process in Nixon's case instead of a compassionate but premature pardon would have helped determine the dividing line between criminal and lawful activity for future Presidents. No doubt a picture of Nixon making license plates at Leavenworth—even though too alien to our history to be desirable, in my opinion—would have been a greater deterrent to future presidential miscreants than pictures of him strolling the beach at San Clemente with King Timahoe, his daily bread assured by substantial appropriations of the people's tax dollars.

Nevertheless, even had each of these legal processes run its full course, Watergate—because it represented something more than a series of crimes and misdemeanors, high and low—would still have raised basic but unanswered questions about the role of the Presidency in our system.

In insisting that we look for more answers, in suggesting that Nixon's exposure and departure were not by themselves sufficient deterrents to future Watergates, I am not advocating a search-and-destroy mission against the Office of the Presidency. I would instead apply in a broader context the words which House Judiciary Committee member James Mann of South Carolina used to support impeachment:

We should strive to strengthen and protect the Presidency. But if there be no accountability, another President will feel free to do as he chooses. The next time there may be no watchman in the night.

2
Was Nixon an Aberrant?

We could forget these close calls of the past and these questions for the future if we could only blame everything on Richard Nixon and his band of second-story men, and assume that their exit from the back door of the White House ended the matter. But that would be the easy way (as Nixon liked to say when declining to do what was right). Nothing would give me greater satisfaction, if I may inject a personal note, than to conclude that the man whose "enemies" list included my name was so gross an aberration on the scale of predictable presidential behavior that his case can be safely ignored. But Nixon kept saying that the charges against him raised fundamental questions about our whole concept of the Presidency; and in my heart I know he's right.

I cannot deny, based upon my own experience with that heady atmosphere in the White House, that the same conditions and motivations that led to Watergate could well recur. The dangers it symbolized did not begin and will not end with Richard Nixon. An overreaction to his singular deeds in the form of drastic structural or institutional alterations would be equally dangerous, as noted later. But, as John Dean said in his famous warning to Nixon, there *is* "a cancer growing in the White House." Cancers being hard to curb completely, this one was not wholly terminated in 1974. I now realize I saw traces of it in 1964. Unless we act, it could reach Orwellian proportions by 1984.

This is not to imply that Gerald Ford is another Nixon. No

one could be another Nixon. But no one knows who will succeed Ford, or who will at any given time be advising him. We do know that, but for the accidents of timing and whim, either Spiro Agnew or John Connally might have succeeded Nixon in the White House. We do know that it is frequently at the very peak of their popularity that Presidents are most likely to misperceive reality and underestimate the need for caution and consultation. (Note the attempted court-packing in 1937, the Bay of Pigs in 1961, the Vietnam invasion in 1965, the Watergate cover-up in 1973, and the pardon of Richard Nixon in 1974.) I accept Mr. Ford's pledges of openness and cooperation as sincere. But, as presidential scholar Thomas Cronin has quoted one of my former White House colleagues as saying, "everybody believes in democracy —until he gets to the White House." [1]

Nor am I implying that Nixon and his defenders were justified in claiming that he did nothing worse than his predecessors. Those who term Nixon and Watergate a culmination of past trends, and those who assert that he was a total aberration, both oversimplify. It is important to sort out what was new and different about Nixon's behavior and what was not.

The high crimes and misdemeanors for which his impeachment was specifically recommended did not, to the best of my knowledge, characterize the conduct of any previous American President. I know of no other President who was personally and directly involved in the cover-up of crimes, the obstruction of justice, and the defiance of those congressional committees, courts, and prosecutors who then investigated

these misdeeds. Earlier Presidents who had Nixon's same ends
in mind—such as assuring their reelection, or isolating their
critics, or stopping leaks—used legitimate means to achieve
those ends, generally out in the open. The scandals of the
Grant and Harding Administrations involved a covert lust for
money, not power; and they were not concentrated in the
White House.

Although Nixon detested the name of John Kennedy, and
tried to blacken it with forged cables, he frequently invoked it
in his own defense in his Watergate speeches and press
conferences. As it became known that he had authorized the
burglarizing of private offices, spent large sums of the taxpayers' money on his personal residences, taped all of his
telephone conversations, and tapped the telephones of White
House correspondents and officials, he tried to imply that
President Kennedy had done all of these. That is simply
untrue.

Nevertheless it is true that many of the *nonimpeachable*
complaints levelled against Nixon could have been levelled
against one or more of his predecessors. He was not the first
President or presidential candidate to receive and dispense
large unreported sums of cash in the course of a campaign, to
obtain information from within the camp of his opponent, to
sanction "dirty trick" campaigning, to use government appointees to seek campaign contributions, or to name Ambassadors and other government appointees from the rankest ranks
of campaign contributors.

Earlier Presidents may not have formally listed their
enemies or urged the Internal Revenue Service to harass

them; but they knew who they were, and could be ruthless and vituperative in dealing with them. All Presidents had their fights with reporters and tried to "manage" the news, at least in the sense of combining timing, charm, and pressure to get their accomplishments highlighted and their mistakes overlooked. I still remember with discomfort those occasions when Presidents Kennedy and Johnson asked me to bawl out friends in the press for stories they did not like.

There is nothing new about incumbent Presidents taking reelection politics into consideration when making governmental decisions or extending governmental benefits. (This is not to be confused with bribery by the milk producers' lobby.) The Nixon Administration's "Project Responsiveness" may have taken this premise to a new extreme; but no President of a democracy is likely to exercise his judgment on economic issues without some attention to their political impact on the interest groups involved.

Several Presidents before Nixon, from Jefferson to Kennedy, impounded appropriated funds, particularly for new weapons systems they regarded as redundant. They may not have permanently impounded as many entire domestic program budgets as frequently or with such obvious disdain for the express will of both Congress and the courts; but it should be noted that they were praised for these impoundments by some of the same people who later said Nixon had no legal right to impound anything.

Most modern Presidents on occasion have lied to the country, deceived Congress, and kept secret some of their doings that should have been public. All have been accused of "interfering" with the executive branch and of inserting their own loyalists into key listening posts at or below the subcabinet level. All chose White House aides at least partly because of their personal service and loyalty to the President. (Certainly I was not named Special Counsel to the President at age 32 because of my long experience at the bar.)

Nearly all White House aides have incurred the resentment of one or more members of the Cabinet, Congress, the bureaucracy, and the press. Ensconced in White House positions and perquisites, "it was easy to lose perspective" for all of us, not only hapless Hugh Sloan and his colleagues under Nixon. Profanity and petty gossip occurred in Oval Office conversations long before the Nixon transcripts had to be sanitized; and the reticent Bebe Rebozo was only the latest of a long line of presidential cronies whose influence and appeal were not discernible by the general public.

Both Kennedy and Johnson defined "national security" to fit their policy objectives, and used the CIA and the armed forces without congressional authorization or sometimes advance knowledge. Johnson developed a concern over protest groups—although not Nixon's obsession—and he placed many of them under surveillance. Given his working relationship with his brother the Attorney General, it seems likely that President Kennedy knew of and implicitly acquiesced in the wiretapping of Martin Luther King, Jr. (as part of an investigation of someone else).

Lyndon Johnson was never accused of evading taxes or using public funds for his private enrichment, but there is no doubt that the various business assets in his wife's name increased amazingly over the many years that he was a full-time public servant. Johnson and Kennedy both invoked executive privilege on occasion. Eisenhower practically copyrighted the term—to the cheers of those now denouncing the doctrine—when he denied certain files to Senator Joseph McCarthy on the basis of some very doubtful law and precedents.

Without question some of these attributes of previous presidential operations are harmful when power is in the wrong hands, but some are bad no matter who rules. All of them pale in comparison to the unauthorized use of the power to initiate war. Without retracing the history and law previously spelled out by the works of Schlesinger and others, it is sufficient to state that the authors of the Constitution clearly intended to reserve to the legislative branch the final authority on any full-scale commitment of American forces to sustained combat abroad. Congress itself has long been derelict in protecting this responsibility, consistently permitting or implicitly ratifying the initiation of foreign hostilities by American Presidents (Vietnam being only the most recent example). Nevertheless, it is clear that the pattern envisioned by the framers was not followed by Presidents prior to Nixon, and equally clear that presidentially authorized wars must be regarded with as much seriousness as the very different kind of problem posed by Watergate.

Indeed the decisions surrounding the 1961 Bay of Pigs invasion, the 1965 escalation of Vietnam, and the 1972–73 Watergate break-in and cover-up have at least some tenuous links. Motivation is not one of them. Although the White

House "plumbers" were allegedly organized initially to deal with national security leaks, the Watergate break-in and cover-up were wholly motivated—unlike the Bay of Pigs and Vietnam operations—by domestic political considerations. Nevertheless all three sets of decisions were born in the cold war age, in which secrecy and national security became national obsessions. It was an age in which the use of covert operations and "dirty tricks" without regard to traditional constitutional processes had been consistently justified as the necessary means of securing national objectives against adversaries who allegedly respected no law or truth. It was also an age in which the President's objectives often became our national objectives on the assumption that time was too short, conditions too tense, and information too tightly held to permit an open debate on matters where papa knows best.

All three sets of decisions also reflected the sense of invincibility and infallibility that too often pervades the White House, especially in the midst or aftermath of a successful election campaign. In addition, all three reflected a kind of gung-ho approach that rejects as "soft" any counsel of caution or reexamination, ignores adverse advice, unfavorable intelligence, and the possibility of failure, and disregards the importance of congressional consent, public opinion, and moral considerations. Surely it is not surprising that any enterprise launched with that spirit is thereafter managed in secret, kept alive with illusions, and justified to the public (when exposed) with half-truths.

Fortunately Kennedy chose to abort the Bay of Pigs invasion before it got out of control, and accepted full blame for its launching (which unfortunately cut off debate about the whole issue of covert operations). But the fallout from this country's long, brutal involvement in Vietnam poisoned much of American society. Massive protests, some of them violent, increased the White House's concern for internal security and its sense of paranoia and isolation, particularly after the invasion of Cambodia. The President's distrust of the press, of the opposition, and even of his own bureaucracy grew. Every news leak caused a fury; every critic had suspect motives. Nixon's creation of his own secret investigative units, drawing upon CIA resources and experience, was the next logical step. Thus are plumbers made, not born.

To be sure, both the Vietnam and Watergate enterprises failed of their own excesses. In both instances, cover-ups not only proved unsuccessful, but also antagonized the press and the citizenry. Under prolonged exposure, both enterprises were revealed to be contrary to our national traditions. An aroused American peace movement helped persuade Johnson to withdraw from the presidential campaign of 1968. An aroused American public helped persuade Nixon to withdraw from the Presidency in 1974. "Watergate," former Secretary of the Interior Walter Hickel has written, "was the Vietnam of the so-called silent majority."

But, despite these tenuous links, the wrongs of Watergate cannot be excused by the wrongs of Vietnam. And the essence of Watergate—the perversion of our political and judicial procedures—struck at the very roots of our liberty at home in a way that wrongful U.S. intervention abroad, however shameful, never could.

Unfortunately, the question of a President's power to initiate war was no more finally settled by Vietnam than the questions of executive privilege and "national security" authority were settled by Watergate. The House Judiciary Committee, aware of congressional complicity in our Indochina ventures, refused to cite Nixon's secret war in Cambodia as an impeachable offense. The Supreme Court refused to rule against presidential war in Indochina, even after the last shred of congressional authority had been withdrawn. Indeed, in the Nixon tapes case, it indicated broad approval for presidentially imposed secrecy in national security matters.

Congress did finally enact in 1973 a new War Powers Act which its proponents argued would curb presidential powers and prevent any more Vietnams. Regrettably it could do the opposite. The Act expressly authorizes a President to initiate new hostilities for 90 days before he needs the consent of Congress. Modern wars can be won or lost in 90 days. If continuing, most of them are still popular at that stage; and, popular or not, Congress traditionally has felt compelled to support troops already in the field. The Constitution did not contemplate a President waging full-scale war with American troops abroad for even one week without authority from the Congress. The new law even specifically exempted from its coverage the conflict then continuing in Indochina. In short, as Senator Tom Eagleton has written of the War Powers Act in its final version:

Congress had answered the President's usurpation of its most solemn power by legitimizing it. The enactment of the war powers bill was the culmination of an era of Congressional surrender.[2]

One other fact links Vietnam with Watergate—their cumulative effect on the mood of the country. Especially but not exclusively among the young, disillusionment and disaffection have steadily risen over the last decade, diminishing hope and confidence in our system, in our institutions, in our parties, and in our politicians. Many college students cannot even remember life under a President whom they respected; and when the nation's best known and most powerful political leader is no longer believed, that erosion of trust is bound to spread to other political establishments. For example: 96 percent of individual incumbent Congressmen seeking reelection in 1972 achieved it, but that same Congress as a body recently earned the approval of only 16 percent of those polled.

This national dispiritedness could in time be even more dangerous to our democracy than another Watergate. Lower political and voting participation, the collapse of our two major political parties, a decline in voluntary compliance with our legal and tax structures, an explosion in the streets of sullen antagonisms—any one of these serious breakdowns in our system, combined with the growing trend toward packaged candidates sold through media manipulation by political technologists, could help pave the way for a nonpolitical "hero" as President not unlike those strongmen who have risen in other countries in the wake of a crisis of the spirit. This peril is not to be lightly dismissed. But it is unlikely to abate fully until the American people are confident that Watergate will not happen again.

Optimists assure us that no President would ever again dare

provoke the kind of public outrage engendered by Watergate. But pessimists remind us that public outrage in this country has a habit of subsiding before long-range reforms are undertaken. Our history has sometimes consisted of national trauma followed by national progress—but that is not an inevitable law. If changes in our approach to the Presidency are to be made, they must be undertaken now, while congressional and public attention is high.

There are disadvantages to reassessing the Presidency in this abnormal period. Once when I thought of the Presidency I saw only Kennedy, and would have mistakenly enlarged the powers of the office accordingly. Today when some think of the Presidency they see only Nixon, and would mistakenly curb its powers accordingly. Emotions may still run too high to permit a careful and objective evaluation of long-standing institutional arrangements. But we cannot ignore the problem. We cannot afford to "put Watergate behind us."

II
The Illusion of Omnipotence

3
The Facade of Unlimited Presidential Power

The first reaction of many a politician to a constitutional crisis is to change the Constitution. It is not always a sound reaction.

In response to the four successive Presidential victories of Franklin Roosevelt, the Republican majorities in both houses of the Eightieth Congress unanimously and vindictively proposed the Twenty-second "no third term" Amendment. They thereby introduced into the Constitution an unnecessary rigidity which Washington and Hamilton had explicitly opposed, which Eisenhower thought "not wholly wise," and which in some future emergency we all may rue. Eight years living on the political bull's-eye will normally be enough for any President and will normally be as long as even an adoring electorate will want him to stay. But the Twenty-second Amendment could easily be repealed in order to provide greater flexibility for some extraordinary period as well as increased political sensitivity in a second term President, without fear of frequent violations of the two term tradition.

At least partly in response to the illness of President Lyndon Johnson at a time when the Vice Presidency was vacant, Congress proposed the Twenty-fifth Amendment. As a result we now have a President never elected by the people (or even considered by his party for that office) but appointed by his discredited predecessor whom he in turn promptly pardoned for any and all crimes. We now have an appointed Vice President, named by the appointed President, who was subject to confirmation (and to far more intense scrutiny than any popularly elected candidate) by a Congress controlled by the opposition party. He will be the third man to hold that post in the course of a single term. We could have also had an impeached President stepping aside for the duration of his Senate trial with neither the Acting President nor the country nor the world knowing with any certainty whether the new man and his policies would last or for how long. Is this an improvement? Admittedly any alternative considered has equal drawbacks; but perhaps we would have done better to leave the Constitution alone, recalling the wise words attributed to John Sherman when Buchanan was fumbling in the White House: "The Constitution already provides for every contingency except a vacancy in the mind of the President."

Nevertheless, after traumas like Watergate, those who think of government in terms of lines and boxes on organizational charts inevitably want the lines redrawn or new boxes created. There is a certain simplistic appeal to this demand for new structures and curbs. We have been subjected to abuses of presidential power; we must therefore reduce that power. If the answer is not a new constitutional amendment, it is a new institutional arrangement, some new set of formal checks and balances to see to it that Watergate never happens again.

In truth some new laws are needed, as will be discussed in Part III of this volume. They may help prevent abuses and excesses. They may help Congress, the courts, and the public reassert their proper roles. But these are not new laws to reduce the principal powers of the Presidency. Those we do not need. Mindful of my erroneously uncritical appraisals of the strong Presidency a decade ago, I am nonetheless as opposed to a reduction in the President's *constitutional* authority as I am to its continued abuse.

Contrary to conventional wisdom, the Presidency has not been given too much power. Over the years that power has increased; and in recent years the American people have suffered outrageous abuses of legal power and witnessed attempted grabs for excessive power. But the actual legitimate power now granted by the Constitution to the Presidency is not unreasonable or dangerous. On the contrary, without funds approved by Congress, without appointees approved by the Senate, without the energetic participation of the permanent bureaucracy, and without the ultimate approval of public opinion, the President can accomplish very little that is of lasting importance.

Inherent Limitations

I realize that the office looks all-powerful from the outside. But it does not appear that way from within. "Every President," John Kennedy wrote in 1963, "must endure a gap between what he would like and what is possible." [1] Earlier he had confessed that "there are greater limitations upon our ability to bring about a favorable result than I had imagined."

This view was not peculiar to Kennedy. Franklin Roosevelt termed Lincoln "a sad man because he couldn't get it all at once. And nobody can." [2] Truman shed crocodile tears over the day that Eisenhower would discover that in his new post he could give few effective commands. Both Johnson and Nixon became bitter over the frustrations of the office.

To be sure, our Presidents themselves (and their speechwriters) are partly responsible for this outside impression of omnipotence. They like the impression made by a ringing presidential declaration that states, with regard to some pressing problem: "I have ordered . . . I have directed . . . I have decided . . ." (Said Gerald R. Ford: "The ethical tone will be what I make it.")

The truth is that Presidents give very few commands or directives. General Alexander Haig told Acting Attorney General William Ruckelshaus, after the Elliot Richardson resignation, that he had to fire Archibald Cox: "Don't you realize your Commander-in-Chief has given you an order?" But most Presidents do not even try to give orders. They rely on persuasion, suggestion, and negotiation. From President Kennedy's file of memoranda to his department and agency heads, for example, the following are typical:

To the Secretary of Agriculture: What would you think of the idea of taking a tour by automobile among the farmers this summer or fall for about ten days . . . ?

To the Secretary of Defense: I was tremendously impressed with the Special Forces Unit in West Germany. However, I am wondering if we are making the best use of this unit. Wouldn't it be a good idea to send them on training missions . . . ?

To the Secretary of the Interior: I am shocked at . . . the spread of polio in the Trust Territories. . . . I would like to have an investigation made into why . . .

To the Director of the Peace Corps: I note that you have plans of increasing the number of Peace Corps Volunteers in . . . North Borneo. I would like you to keep in mind the importance of Latin America. . . . Do we not [already] have as many in the Philippines as we have in all of the Latin American countries?

Nor do Presidents make very many unilateral decisions—at least not in the sense of writing their own free, full conclusions on a clean slate. They make choices. They select options. They exercise judgments. But this is all limited by the pressures and precedents of others and by the information and resources available.

All new Presidents soon discover that their control of events is not equal to their responsibility, to their campaign promises, or to the voters' excessive and contradictory expectations. They are all discouraged to discover how little they can actually cut from their predecessor's domestic budget to make room for their new programs or promised tax reductions. They are disturbed to learn how little they can do, and how long it takes, to curb inflation, unemployment, urban blight, poverty, or other popular targets of campaign oratory. Lyndon Johnson may have declared war on poverty, and Gerald Ford may have declared war on inflation; but they had to depend on Congress for their weapons and on the civil service for their battalions.

Finally, new Presidents are appalled by their inability to obtain the information they require. "In the future," President Kennedy acidly added on a memorandum to one of his agency heads, "I wish you would keep the White House informed in advance of actions which may later involve it." Lyndon Johnson, according to one of his former Budget Bureau aides, William Carey, tried for years to get the Bureau to assign "five of the best men you have to drag advance information out of the agencies about impending decisions and actions."[3] But he never got it.

"I don't think people understand," said C. Jackson Grayson after his 1971–73 stint as Price Commissioner,

that really a lot of what's done at the central level is done on an awful lot of guesswork . . . [or] how many decisions we had to make where we did not really understand what was going to happen. . . .

Those of us who had worked at the "central" level understood. I saw two Presidents required on more than one occasion by limits on their time, resources, and information to take actions or to make pronouncements which were one part improvisation, one part a response to headlines, and one part [expletive deleted]. Contrary to the prevailing view, life in the White House is not a series of dramatic crises but of unending daily efforts to keep the machinery of government running without too many breakdowns or explosions.

Each post–World War II President—at least prior to Ford—preferred to concentrate his efforts on foreign affairs, where the opportunities to appear statesmanlike without antagonizing voters were believed to be greater. But here, too, the choices are limited. Foreign leaders habitually assume, President Kennedy once remarked, that the President can change the minds and course of every country—except their own. In truth most of the pieces on the international board are not his to move, nor can all the vaunted apparatus of secret cables and intelligence-gathering ever assure him that he knows enough to choose the right move.

The high level intelligence briefings and reports I reviewed in my White House days were, to put it politely, of uneven quality. Some facts garnered through ingenious technology were both reliable and useful. Some estimates of future developments were well-documented, well-hedged, and already well-known. And some reports were best summed up by the enlightened verse provided several years ago by Charles Burton Marshall:

Absolute knowledge we really have none
But a secret informant's stenographer's son
Overheard a policeman, while walking his beat,
Remark to a laborer crossing the street
That certain unspecified Portuguese Jews
Had wind of a sailor in Newport News
Who had learned while abroad, from an undisclosed source,
There's doubt on the size of the enemy's force,
And the prospect's unclear, to be candid and terse,
The crisis may soon be made better or worse . . .

Institutional Limitations

The Departments and Career Service
In addition to these inherent limitations on presidential power, there are four outside institutions capable of limiting that power: the rest of the executive branch, the press, Congress, and the judiciary.

The casual observer assumes that the executive branch is a monolith controlled by the President. It is nothing of the kind. To a White House staffer like McGeorge Bundy, it "more nearly resembles a collection of badly separated principalities." The President, as Richard Neustadt has written, is more clerk than commander within the executive branch. As already noted, he rarely orders but requests, prods, and persuades. Some but not all of his requests are willingly accepted and implemented by some but not all of those who receive them, including his own department heads.

Obviously most department heads do not take office with any notion of limiting the President's power, particularly in recent times when few Cabinet members have enjoyed any political base of their own. They owe all to the President; they take office eager to help and support him. But in office they also depend upon Congress and anywhere from two to eight of its committees in each house for their legislative authority and funds. They depend upon their career personnel experts for advice and ideas. They depend upon the particular constituents of their departments—farmers, unions, builders, businessmen or whatever—for public and political support. Only the Department of State lacks a true domestic constituency of its own; and the career Foreign Service's traditional fear of making a mistake that will incur the wrath of either Congress or our allies has given that Department a built-in timidity that frustrates every President anyway.

Recent Presidents, sensing that their major appointees could slip out of their orbit, have mistakenly tried to compensate by establishing still more functions in the White House or Executive Offices, as discussed later. But they still must depend for the implementation of most policies largely on departments and bureaus established, empowered, funded, instructed, and restricted by Congress. The President is an important source of support to the departments, but not their only one.

Thus the executive branch will never be run like a streamlined business enterprise. President Kennedy could not induce his Secretary of Defense to accept his (Kennedy's) first choice for Secretary of the Navy; or persuade his Secretary of the Treasury to propose or accept any important balance-of-payments innovations; or get his Secretary of the Air Force to abandon the B-70; nor did he have the authority to order the Federal Deposit Insurance Corporation to prohibit race discrimination in housing financed by the banks which it insured. Any chief executive of a private business corporation has greater power over his subordinates than does the President of the United States.

President Nixon, with the encouragement of corporate graduates like Fred Malek, tried to compensate for these weaknesses by relentlessly centralizing all decision-making in the White House and installing puppets in the domestic departments and agencies. The result even before Watergate was confusion, inaction, and ineptitude in a whole series of policy and program areas where the departments, still indispensable in a diverse and interdependent society, failed to function properly.

To be sure, the President can within limits fire an incompetent or recalcitrant appointee (or, what is worse, promote him to federal judge or ambassador, as JFK occasionally did). But some key positions have fixed terms or tenure; and for those that do not, no President can be certain of finding a preferable substitute for the appointee he fires.

Federal jobs, it should be added, are not a major instrument of presidential power. Now that the Postal Service has been made as efficient as the telephone company by becoming a quasi-private enterprise, there remain some 2.8 million federal civilian employees. Of these, less than 7,000 are outside the Civil Service system and only 522 are considered executive-level appointees. And compensation alone is not sufficient to induce qualified men and women to accept the burdens that come with these jobs. (Moreover, as William Howard Taft remarked, for every post a President fills he creates "nine enemies and one ingrate.") Lyndon Johnson complained privately that too many of his policy positions went by default to career civil servants who were willing, available, and technically competent but had no "fire in their bellies."

These career civil servants, whatever the state of their bellies, are indispensable but not always amenable. Over the years they watch Presidents come and go. They see bold new programs rise and fall. They know they have more expertness, more contacts in the field, and more continuity than the President does. They control most of the flow of information to the White House and, in the long run, most of the policy initiatives and implementation as well. Many of them have survived by cautious adherence to the tried and true. Many are concerned primarily about their own priorities, prerogatives, jurisdiction, and autonomy, and will endlessly delay or dilute any new presidential move that upsets them.

White House assistants inquiring into their departmental areas are regarded as intruders. The Kennedy White House, on the whole impressed by the talent in the career services, sought to maintain harmonious relations with them. Nevertheless, we sometimes paid a price by unduly deferring to agency wishes or in not being kept fully informed by agency experts.

The Army's insistence on providing both Kennedy and Johnson with its own version of events in Vietnam was obviously harmful. Internal Revenue's insistence on rejecting Nixon's enemies list was obviously beneficial. The bureaucracy's check on presidential power can clearly be either—the fact remains that it is a check.

The Press

The check provided by the bureaucracy is frequently exercised in informal alliance with another power center that does not show up on the government organization charts, but nevertheless acts as a practical limitation on presidential power; the press. A frequently used device for collaboration between bureaucracy and press is the executive "leak," defining that term in its broadest sense to cover the publication of any information from an anonymous executive branch source that the President would not have wanted published. (Items he welcomes, even if obtained in the same way from the same source, are "stories," not "leaks.") No matter how powerful a President may think he is, leaks occur every day of the year.

There is no single explanation. Frequently the leak is a means of exposing to public criticism a White House proposal or procedure that the leaker wants to weaken or at least let the reporter know he opposed. Sometimes it is a means of gratifying the leaker's ego, by demonstrating that he is "in the know" or by currying favor with the reporter. Sometimes it is extracted by reportorial guile or artful questioning. Occasionally it is mere rumor, guesswork, or invention concocted by the leaker to serve personal or jurisdictional ends. An amazing number of people in Washington find it impossible to refer reporters to other sources, or to keep legitimate confidences, or to know when to be available or willing to comment, or to know how to say "I don't know" even when that happens to be true.

Because every White House tries to keep far too much secret, as will be discussed later, leaks generally protect the public interest more than they harm it. True, they may prove embarrassing, upsetting, or irritating to the President. (In a note to Secretary of the Air Force Eugene Zuckert in 1962, President Kennedy observed that *Time* magazine quoted Zuckert as saying to McNamara that "the tone and pace of our space effort were not right." Kennedy sardonically added:

I do not know how *Time* secured this quotation, but I would be interested in having your suggestions as to how we can improve the tone and pace of our program.)

Leaks may also interfere with a President's timing, with his desire to check all bases and mobilize all support before disclosure, with his penchant for surprise or melodrama, or with his need to have some infant idea matured and strengthened before its enemies can attack it. But these inconveniences and irritations are minor compared to the leak's value in checking excessive presidential secrecy or unwise presidential plans.

Most White House aides with experience in Washington recognize the futility of keeping very many major decisions secret very long. Thus the constant threat of involuntary disclosure substantially increases the amount of voluntary disclosure. It also reduces the temptation to undertake anything that the President would not enjoy reading about on the front page of the *Washington Post* the next day.

All this is part of the press's oversight function regarding the federal government. It exercises that function, as every President will testify, with vigor and persistence—often more so than Congress. When the press's attitude toward Ford turned 180 degrees after his pardon of Nixon, complaint was heard to the effect that there is something unpleasant or improper about the press being constantly in an adversary relationship with the President. On the contrary, I shudder to think what could happen if the enormous powers at the disposal of each were ever combined in total harmony.

Protected at least in theory against government intrusion by the First Amendment and a sometimes independent FCC, protected at least in most cases against forced disclosures of confidential sources by statutory and common-law shields, and protected against virtually any libel suit from a government official by the Supreme Court's ruling in *The New York Times Co.* v. *Sullivan* and its progeny,[4] the Washington press is a powerful force with which every President must contend.

This has its drawbacks. The power to make accusations in public print or over the public airwaves carries with it the same dangers of recklessness, prejudice, and corruption that accompany any other grant of tremendous power. It was a heady experience to help bring down a Vice President and President within a year, and it would not have been unnatural for some 1974 Washington reporters, thus having become accustomed to the taste of blood, to look for fresh victims.

No Washington news office is totally free from committing errors which, once in the files, are more likely to be repeated indefinitely than corrected. Most Washington reporters, in Eugene McCarthy's phrase, seek stories like crows on a telephone wire, hopping on and off topics in droves. Few recognize any right of privacy for government officials or any confidential privilege other than their own. Most correspondents and columnists are better able to voice criticism than to accept it. Nevertheless the increased need for a freer flow of information to the public, and the increased danger of unaccountable power in the Presidency, clearly justify the more aggressive reporting and investigative journalism of the last decade. Irresponsible journalists can hurt; but irresponsible Presidents can destroy.

Presidents (and Vice Presidents) who have tried to undercut the power of the press directly have all come out second best. The President can "go to the country" on television to circumvent the press—but not very often if the public is to remain interested, and not very successfully if his credibility has been impaired. He can go over a reporter's head to his publisher—but that only backfires, as JFK discovered in the case of David Halberstam. He can dominate the headlines, time his announcements, and attempt in other limited ways previously mentioned to "manage" the news, but only to the extent that his words are backed by adequate reserves of that precious coin of the political realm, credibility—which is very different from publicity or popularity.

He can avoid press conferences for long periods, as Nixon did—but that only hurts his own cause. It denies him an invaluable opportunity to communicate directly and effectively to the public and to the rest of his government; and it also denies him the opportunity to find out more about his own administration (which preparation for a press conference inevitably produces). The press is hurt less. It will still fill its news columns and television tapes with whatever it can find or hear.

To both the President and the press, the other appears all too powerful. In fact, each reminds the other that success with the public over the long run is dependent upon a truthful and responsible record.

Congress

The principal limitations on presidential power intended by the authors of the Constitution are those exercised by Congress and the courts. Both institutions, as will be discussed later, must alter their overly deferential approach to the Presidency if they are to hold its power accountable. Neither, as noted earlier, covered itself with sufficient glory early enough in Watergate to reassure us that the status quo is sufficient. Nevertheless, anyone under the misapprehension that the President has virtually unlimited powers is ignoring the very real power the other two branches hold.

Most members of Congress, as does the general public, consider the legislative branch to be a loose collection of 535 individuals, divided into two parties in two houses and over 300 committees, subcommittees, and special committees, confronting one united and powerful presidential establishment. They await the President's budget, his legislative agenda, and his reports on the economy and the State of the Union. They see him as commanding far greater resources, expert assistance, and public acclaim. As Congressman Don Edwards quipped concerning the House Judiciary Committee's inability to force President Nixon to turn over tapes or do anything else:

He's got the Army, Navy and Air Force, and all we've got is Ken Harding [the House Sergeant-at-Arms].

But that is not the way we saw the balance of power from the Kennedy White House. We saw 535 separate skeptics, most of whom owed the President nothing and were far more concerned about their own interests, pressures, and prerogatives than his. The number of different committees and subcommittees on which they served merely reminded us of the number of hurdles a bill must clear, and of the exorbitant amount of time Cabinet members must spend testifying and preparing to testify on "the Hill."

We may not have had the national party platform framed on every White House office wall, but we did at least recognize basic national commitments from the campaign that meant little or nothing to the members of either party in Congress. The annual congressional appropriations process (and, for roughly one-third of the budget, an annual authorization process as well) made long-range presidential planning difficult. The biennial congressional election process made consistent support of presidential proposals doubtful. The quiet web of relationships between powerful committee or subcommittee chairmen and career bureau chiefs made many presidential budget and policy decisions meaningless. We knew about the sweetheart contract which the FBI had with Capitol Hill; it took us a little longer to learn about those of the Bureau of Reclamation, the Passport Office, the Forest Service, the Park Service, the Army Engineers, and several others.

In short, when we looked at Congress from the Kennedy White House, we saw power—particularly the power to limit presidential power. When he had served in Congress, JFK once told me, he envied the Presidency as a citadel of power; but once in the Presidency, he realized how much power Congress truly had.

Congress has the right to establish new agencies and abolish old ones in the executive branch, to withhold confirmation from the President's appointees, to confer additional powers on his subordinates or remove existing powers from them, to alter the terms of eligibility for their offices, and to protect them from removal. It can conduct investigational or educational hearings on every aspect of executive branch conduct, subpoena executive branch witnesses, cite them for perjury if they testify falsely, and cite them for contempt if they refuse to testify at all. It can reject, ignore, or amend the President's legislative and budget requests, withhold funds he needs, impose conditions he does not like, add to his budget more funds than he wants, override his vetoes, and limit the numbers and salaries of his White House aides.

It can prevent ratification of his treaties, block his use of the

armed forces, and subject him to resolutions of censure and (as
we now know with certainty) impeachment. It can narrow the
conditions under which executive privilege is claimed and the
conditions upon which executive agreements are signed. It can
initiate legislation and lawsuits in opposition to the President's
interests. It can with difficulty but in time halt virtually any
presidential activity it desires to halt.

To be sure, some of these rights have atrophied with disuse,
some were bypassed by Nixon, and some should never be
pushed to extremes without unusual provocation, because they
could shut the government down. And to be sure, it is far
easier for the two houses of Congress to deny to a President the
affirmative action he seeks from them, as in JFK's case, than it
is to block or undo action which the President takes or to
compel action which he refuses to take, as in Nixon's case.
Nevertheless, real power is there, and it is enormous power if
used.

No President likes congressional power. Legend has it that
Andrew Jackson selected the site of the Treasury Department
building to the East of the White House to avoid looking out
at the Capitol. But every White House knows the power is
there. Every modern President creates a legislative liaison
staff. He invites the leaders of Congress to breakfast, the
committee chairmen to state dinners, the new members to tea.
He offers favors and jobs for their constituents, grants and
contracts for their districts, speeches and pictures for their
campaigns. All that helps, but not very much.

He can veto bills, but not too many without antagonizing
the nation, inducing Congress to attach key legislation to

appropriations or other essential bills and risking a governmental stalemate. He can *threaten* to veto bills, which gives him a tool for trading or modifying legislation. He can make bargains with powerful committee chairmen but rarely with Congress itself—because, since the days when Texans Lyndon Johnson in the Senate and Sam Rayburn in the House effectively corralled the members of their respective houses, there have been no legislative leaders who could assure delivery of their side of a bargain. He can take congressmen into his confidence—but, with such exceptions as the Joint Committee on Atomic Energy and the Armed Services and Appropriations Subcommittees overseeing the CIA, most congressional committees are unwilling or unable to keep confidential much of the executive information entrusted to them.

The President can try to fight Congress by going to the people, and sometimes he should, but that has limited possibilities. He can try to ignore or defy congressional power, but only until stopped by the courts or by Congress itself—and that is now more likely. He can expand his power, as discussed later, in a real or self-manufactured emergency—but new legislation should make that more difficult. He can, if elected by an imposing majority accompanied by a landslide for his party in Congress, work his legislative will quickly and massively in the months that immediately follow. But those opportunities (as FDR and LBJ discovered) are rare and short-lived, as legislative coalitions realign themselves from issue to issue.

It is true that Nixon and to some extent Johnson worried

less about congressional power than their predecessors. But this was not because they usurped the powers of Congress as much as it was because the members of Congress failed to exercise their own powers.

Hubert Humphrey once remarked in the Senate:

We are fearful men. We will not even provide [for ourselves] a parking lot. And yet we will provide for the Executive Branch of government marble halls.

But in light of Congress's swollen staff and facilities,[5] the real fear was of challenging executive power, not incurring taxpayer retaliation. Most members of Congress went along with sweeping military resolutions and appropriations, with secret executive agreements, with the transfer of departmental operations to Nixon aides who were subject neither to confirmation nor interrogation, and with the expansion of impoundments and executive privilege. They voted new powers and discretion for the President, added new functions to the Executive Office, and confirmed most appointees with hardly a question. What they did not hand over to the President, they acquiesced in his taking. As Congressman Donald Fraser summed up early in the debate over the War Powers Act,

Congress has all the controls it could ever need. All it lacks is the guts to use them.

It still has all those controls. It has repealed many of its most sweeping grants of power and prohibited impoundments without its consent. It also has now a new Budget Control Act and a new Office of Technological Assessment which have considerable potential for improving its bargaining position with the executive branch, particularly if the President is legislation-oriented. Its members are increasingly young, better educated, better staffed, more specialized, and both dedicated and competent, as the televised sessions of the House Judiciary Committee demonstrated.

Changes in Congress's approach are required, along with some new legislation, as will be set forth in Chapter 6. It needs those guts even more than it needs that parking lot. But too much power is there for anyone to believe that the President is all-powerful in relation to Congress; and no constitutional amendment or structural reduction in presidential power is required for a reassertion of Congress's constitutional role as a principal check on the Presidency.

The Courts

The final institutional limitation on the power of the Presidency is the judicial branch. That curb also needs more vigorous exercise, as detailed later. But there can be no doubt that the power to curb is there.

This was first made clear in 1803 in *Marbury* v. *Madison*.[6] John Marshall, speaking for a unanimous Supreme Court, strayed beyond the requirements of the case to make clear that the judiciary was empowered to review, and thus test against the Constitution, not only legislative measures but also acts of the Executive. In another case that should be of current interest, he ruled the following year that obedience to a presidential order does not immunize the obedient official from legal liability if that order is unlawful.[7]

While the courts have been more willing in the 170 years that followed to challenge legislative rather than executive actions, another unanimous Supreme Court last July reaffirmed, in *U.S.* v. *Nixon*,[8] John Marshall's very words:

It is emphatically the province and duty of the Judicial Department to say what the law is.

That judicial power is not to be shared with anyone. No President is entitled to decide the constitutionality of his own actions.

Nixon's lawyers in the tapes case argued that "the President has *his* obligations under the Constitution. . . ." They argued that "law as to the President has to be applied in a Constitutional way which is different than [as applied to] anyone else." His former Secretary of the Treasury John Connally opined that "There are times when the President of the United States would be right in not obeying a decision of the Supreme Court." Nevertheless, even Nixon, after considering that course, felt compelled to abide by the Supreme Court's decision.

So did Jefferson, Madison, Jackson, Lincoln, both Roosevelts, Wilson, and Truman, all of whom chafed at rulings that frustrated their programs. No President has ever defied a Supreme Court order, Andrew Jackson's famous rhetoric (about an order not directed against him)[9] to the contrary notwithstanding, not even in cases involving national emergency powers. (It should be noted, however, that the Supreme

Court ruling against Nixon was the first which affirmatively ordered a President personally to do something.)

No court, to be sure, can determine how the President exercises his constitutional functions. The actions of his political agents in executing his legal discretion, said Marshall in *Marbury*, "are only politically examinable." But the performance or nonperformance of those constitutional functions is subject to judicial review.[10]

Thus the courts have placed limits on the President's powers to seize industrial plants as Commander-in-Chief,[11] on his authority to regulate commerce in national economic emergencies,[12] on his authority to impose embargoes[13] or prize courts[14] during international conflict or military law during civil insurrections,[15] on his ability to dismiss independent agency commissioners,[16] and on his control over executive branch personnel [17] and contractors.[18]

More recently, they have denied that his authority to conduct foreign affairs and as Commander-in-Chief gave him the inherent power to enjoin newspaper publication of "leaked" government documents,[19] to impose an unauthorized import surcharge[20] or to suspend the provisions of the Bill of Rights with respect to wiretaps or burglaries.[21] They have overturned his attempt to use a pocket veto during a brief congressional recess,[22] blocked his impoundment of congressionally appropriated funds,[23] halted his blocking of a congressionally mandated pay raise for federal employees,[24] slowed his dismantling of a congressionally authorized program,[25] and rejected his claim of absolute "executive privilege" of confidentiality for all presidential communications.[26]

A determination of the precise limits of executive privilege awaits future court review. But at least it is now clear that any claim of executive privilege can be subject to court review, and that the privilege does not extend to presidential communications or conversations regarding political activities (conceded by Nixon's lawyer under questioning by the Supreme Court); or to criminal activities (the narrow case before the Court in *U.S.* v. *Nixon*); or to impeachment proceedings (according to at least a narrow majority of the House Judiciary Committee in its third Article of Impeachment against Nixon). Nor do executive branch communications that do not involve the President or his official duties and decisions in foreign or military affairs seem likely to be privileged under the *Nixon* case rationale.

As will be discussed in more detail later, these judicially imposed limitations on the Presidency are not as restrictive or as numerous as they might be. Nevertheless, they negate the notion of an all-powerful President. Nor can any President safely assume on the basis of the Nixon pardon that a different standard of justice applies at his level and that the courts will not proceed against him personally. John Marshall, during the initial proceeding against Aaron Burr, held that his cousin, President Jefferson, was not immune from the issuance of a subpoena.[27] The Supreme Court in 1974 did not disturb (or discuss one way or another in its opinion) the grand jury's decision to name President Nixon as an unindicted co-conspirator. Special Prosecutor Jaworski had felt it best to warn the Watergate grand jury that the question of indicting the President was unsettled and that Nixon's guilt was thus best left to Congress (lest it muddle the cover-up case in the courts). But nothing in the Constitution expressly bars the criminal indictment of a sitting President before impeachment any more than it does that of a sitting judge. "We conclude," said the Court of Appeals in the case of Judge Otto Kerner,

> that whatever immunities or privileges the Constitution confers for the purpose of assuring the independence of the co-equal branches of government, they do not exempt the members of those branches 'from the operation of the ordinary criminal laws.' Criminal conduct is not part of the necessary functions performed by public officials. Punishment for that conduct will not interfere with the legitimate operations of a branch of government.[28]

Although the Solicitor General in his brief on Vice President Agnew sought to distinguish the position of the President, his basic argument applied equally to both offices. "Since the Framers knew how to, and did, spell out immunity, the natural inference is that no immunity exists where none is mentioned." [29]

No, Presidents sitting, standing, or running away do not have unlimited power, and it should not be necessary to indict one to demonstrate that fact. Nor *should* their powers be unlimited. But neither in the light of these limitations do their legitimate constitutional powers, as distinct from the abuses thereof, need to be further reduced. The overwhelming proportion of Presidents since Jackson who have been foreclosed from more than one full term by public or party rejection, ill health, or death can hardly encourage future occupants of that office to assume that they are all-powerful.

They would do better to recollect, as President Kennedy did when he reflected upon the office, Shakespeare's account of the exchange between the boastful Owen Glendower and the cynical Henry Hotspur:

Glendower: I can call spirits from the vasty deep!

Hotspur: Why, so can I, or so can any man; But will they come when you call for them?

Sometimes they do, Mr. President. But not so often as one thinks.

4
The Myth of the Strong Nixon Presidency

The tenure of Richard Nixon, many liberals now say, refutes their previously cherished doctrine that the strong Presidency is the best Presidency. Watergate, they now believe, was the inevitable culmination of the last 40 years. Thus my unfashionable insistence that presidential power is neither unchecked nor excessive will seem proof enough to some that I have learned nothing from the past decade.

But the Nixon Presidency is not, in my view, convincing evidence of the need to reduce or restructure the Office of the President. The Nixon White House may have authorized, condoned, or engaged in burglaries, perjury, illegal surveillance, the abuse of Internal Revenue files, and the other activities cited by the House Judiciary Committee; but Nixon did not actually possess the power—the *legal right*—to do so. Such activities were illegal abuses of legitimate power granted to the President, or attempted usurpations of power withheld from the President. They were not instances of powers that must now be withdrawn from the President, because he did not possess them then and does not possess them now. Additional legal curbs would not have prevented Watergate. This argument is not a semantic quibble over the term "presidential power," but is central to an understanding of Watergate's meaning for the Presidency.

Equally important, if these events are to be kept in perspective, is recognition of the fact that Nixon largely failed. As noted, he came frighteningly close to succeeding. But the notion of an all-powerful Nixon Presidency is based in large part on audacious assertions of power which were ultimately not upheld. There is no doubt that lasting success in that wide-ranging series of attempts, had it been achieved, would have broadened the powers of the Presidency far beyond all precedent, reason, and constitutional limits. In that sense, when Nixon and his attorneys argued that the future of the Presidency was at stake in his case, they were right. But nearly all of those attempts were in the end rejected or abandoned, largely as the result of his own heavy-handed ineptitude:

• Had Mr. Nixon succeeded in imposing his concept of "executive privilege" as set forth by Attorney General Richard Kleindienst to Congress in April 1973 (asserting that not one of the 2.5 million employees of the executive branch or any former employee could be directed by Congress, the FBI, a court, or a grand jury to supply testimony or documents if the President in his sole and unreviewable discretion decided otherwise),[1] then Congress could not possibly conduct in a meaningful way its function of overseeing the executive departments. The equal application of law by the courts could have been halted by presidential whim. But that interpretation, inconsistent with existing statutes and judicial decisions, was not accepted by Congress, was rejected by the courts, and was finally abandoned by the President.

• Had Mr. Nixon succeeded in imposing his concept of inherent "national security" powers, as set forth in the Senate Watergate testimony of his aide John Ehrlichman (who refused even to draw the line at presidentially ordered murder under that doctrine), then the end of American democracy as we know it would have been at hand. Neither the files, nor the phone, nor the person or premises of any citizen suspected of disagreement with a President's policies on external or internal security—or suspected of professional or personal contact with such a dissenter—would have been secure. But Judges Gesell and Sirica rejected this doctrine, and the House Judiciary Committee deemed its exercise grounds for impeachment.

• Had Mr. Nixon succeeded in getting the House Judiciary Committee to adopt a narrow theory of impeachment based only on major indictable crimes, or had he been upheld in his defiance of relevant committee subpoenas, then that ultimate legislative weapon by which the Constitution holds Presidents accountable would have been rendered virtually useless. But the committee neither adopted nor acted in accordance with this narrow constitutional theory. A majority of members specifically stated that impeachment was also based on his violation of his constitutional oath and obligations, not alone on federal criminal statutes; and a too-narrow majority also included among its Articles of Impeachment the President's rejection of Judiciary Committee subpoenas seeking material which existing evidence indicated was related to impeachable conduct.

• Finally, had Mr. Nixon succeeded in his argument that he could interpret the Constitution for himself or as Chief Law Enforcement Officer decide which crimes to report, or had he succeeded in concealing from Congress, the courts, and the public the Watergate horrors and his own unlawful activities, or had he succeeded in staying in office after public exposure of these activities, then future Presidents would have felt still less accountable and more willing to usurp and monopolize power. But he did not succeed. He may have escaped prison through a pardon from his successor, but he did not escape punishment.

Still other vain Nixon efforts could be cited: his attempt through the unprecedented impoundment of appropriated funds to nullify legislative authority over spending (largely rejected by the courts to date); his attempt through the premature dismantling of the Office of Economic Opportunity to nullify congressional mandates (also rejected by the courts); his attempt to restrict congressional oversight of departmental operations by making department heads White House counsellors and creating a super-cabinet without legislative sanction (largely abandoned under Watergate pressure); the Huston Plan for a far-reaching and illegal new domestic intelligence effort (abruptly terminated by J. Edgar Hoover's objections); and the injunction against the *New York Times* and the *Washington Post* for publishing the Pentagon Papers (quickly terminated by the courts). No doubt some of these failures might have been successes had the Watergate break-in and cover-up not been exposed. But the fact remains that they failed.

In short, Richard Nixon is not proof of excessive powers in the Presidency, for he was ultimately found to lack such powers. His misconduct, concluded the House Judiciary Committee with respect to its second Article of Impeachment, "cannot be justified under the most expansive view of the discretionary or inherent powers of a President."

In fact, I will go further and assert that Nixon was not even one of our strong Presidents. I realize he was generally so regarded and sought to be so regarded. I acknowledge that he succeeded in altering the ideological balance on the Supreme Court and embarked upon important new relationships with China and the U.S.S.R. But he was not in the mold of Jefferson, Jackson, Lincoln, the two Roosevelts, and others.

Those whom history regards as strong Presidents had strong convictions about great national purposes which went well beyond skill in public relations and political campaigning. An attempt to monopolize power, close off dissent, and place oneself above the law in defiance of all other institutions is not what is meant by a strong Presidency. Excessive secrecy and seclusiveness are not signs of greatness; nor are an imperious tone, an arrogant and swollen staff, grandiose homes with tax-paid improvements, or guards in comic-opera uniforms.

Nixon constantly sought more power, but was notably unskilled in utilizing the power he already had. He doggedly acquired leadership, but was not a leader in the sense of following up on his messages, laboring diligently with Congress and the bureaucracy, cultivating a broader base of followers, and articulating the issues of the day in something other than generalities. According to one of his carly White House aides, Daniel P. Moynihan, who was disappointed by the President's failure to fight for his family assistance proposals:

. . . initial thrusts were rarely followed up with a sustained . . . second and third order of advocacy . . . the impression was allowed to arise . . . [that] the President really wasn't behind them.

Nixon shrank from the press, excessively feared the opposition, and secluded himself from Congress. "Nobody is a friend of ours . . . let's face it," he told John Dean four months after his massive reelection victory. Every President is in danger of isolation behind that iron gate, surrounded by deferential aides. But few have been as isolated as Nixon or have misperceived reality so badly as a result. He was, said Senator Barry Goldwater, "the most complete loner I've ever known. The man operates all by himself." That is not the mark of a President who is comfortable with power.

Politically and personally insecure, Nixon wanted mostly unknowns and mediocrities in his final Cabinet, discouraging (with the exception of Henry Kissinger) any show of innovation that might outshine him. This was in contrast with those strong Presidents (not all of them, to be sure) who were delighted to have the lustre of a George Marshall or the independence of a Harold Ickes on their team.

Nixon took no action to fill many key vacancies for inordinately long periods. He took no direct interest in major economic problems or in several important but undramatic areas of foreign policy. Preoccupation with Watergate pressures took a special toll in his last year in office. He was not even awake, much less present, when in his name two members of the National Security Council ordered a worldwide nuclear alert of uncertain necessity during the Mideast conflict of October 1973. Contrast that with John Kennedy's insistence eleven years earlier during the Cuban missile crisis that even small steps involving major risk were to be reviewed by him before the moment of implementation arrived.

Substituting appearance for substance, Nixon as President offered little consistency of direction. His economic policies shot from one polar position to the other. His energy programs went through a welter of conflicting and overlapping policies, agencies, and chiefs. (Even his notable efforts for a dialogue with China and détente with Russia, while clearly exercises of presidential power, were antithetical to his entire previous political career.) Elaborate machinery installed in the Executive Offices for planning and coordination produced comparatively little of either.

He imposed wage and price controls after Congress authorized them against his wishes. He did not fulfill his pledge to end all U.S. military involvement in Indochina until almost five years after taking office. Even then Congress had to order a halt to the bombing of Cambodia. Like Kennedy, he had difficulty with a Congress opposed to many of his programs. But, unlike Kennedy, he did not personally work to woo the Congress, to educate the public, to mobilize his partisans, and to rely on the positive results of give-and-take instead of defiance and veto.

Unlike Roosevelt, who realigned the Democratic Party into a national majority, Nixon gravely weakened his party. He ignored it entirely in the establishment of separate machinery for his own reelection, refusing to share the enormous funds raised through his efforts and agents. When things went wrong, he purported to accept responsibility but not blame. Those are not the characteristics of a strong leader.

According to his former aide, Herb Klein, Nixon allowed his sense of values to be distorted by the likes of Haldeman, Ehrlichman, and Colson. Yet there was nothing strong about these close advisers, "seduced" in Senator Sam Ervin's words, "by a lust for political power." White Houses in earlier days may have been the scene of other forms of seduction but not this kind of corruption. The Watergate transcripts show not a strong, decisive President in command of his own staff—any strong President would have promptly cleaned house from top to bottom—but a weak and muddled cynic. His judgments on the importance of Watergate, on the strategy to be followed, and on the responses to be made, were even for a guilty man unrealistic in the extreme.

No doubt my view of the Nixon Presidency is distorted by partisan bias. But it is primarily his partisan detractors who cite him as an argument against any more strong Presidents; and I do not think the record shows that he was a strong President. Unfortunately history has heretofore rated as our best Presidents those who won notable victories over Congress, the Constitution, or other countries in times of war or national emergency. I would hope that the Nixon experience would cause a reexamination of this standard, and enable future Presidents to be judged more by the strength of their wisdom, by the talent they attract, and by their ability to lead through comity instead of coercion.

Even Watergate itself reflected not excessive strength, as commonly stated, but excessive weakness—weak men operating in an atmosphere of frustration instead of power. The Nixon White House, already discomfited by its inability to make good on its promises to cut the budget, curb inflation, reduce crime, and end the Indochina war, was further outraged by its inability to stem leaks from within the executive branch itself. The staff felt "resentment and frustration," Jeb Magruder testified, "unable to deal with issues on a legal basis." Uncertain of the bureaucracy, unable to get J. Edgar Hoover's support for the Huston plan, unwilling to disclose its objectives to a Congress and a press it could not command, it thereupon established its own surreptitious investigative force. Unable to get the facts it wanted on Ellsberg, unable to trust some of its own White House employees, uncertain of winning a fair contest with the Democrats, it stooped to repeated violations of the law. This was weakness, not strength.

Thus it makes no sense to further weaken or disperse presidential power in response to Watergate actions that were already illegal, or to increase this atmosphere of frustration for future Presidents on the assumption that Nixon was a strong President.

Nor is it correct to cite the misdeeds of Richard Nixon as the culmination of a long institutional evolution which steadily increased the powers of the Presidency. Those powers have indeed increased, and Watergate was in a sense facilitated by that trend. But the existence of the Nixon Presidency was more the result of political accident than institutional evolution. Without the two Kennedy assassinations, the choice in 1968 might well have been different; and even a minuscule shift in the popular vote in 1968 would have elected a very un-Nixon kind of President, a man not in the least reclusive, or shy with the press, or remote from Congress. (Complaint would have been heard instead about President Humphrey's unfair advantage in holding hour-long press conferences twice a week.)

We should not minimize the evils of Watergate. But they are not the evils of a strong Presidency, and strong Presidents with strong commitments are not necessarily evil. Structural reductions in presidential authority would be the wrong answer to the wrong problem. "The power of the executive establishment," stated former Special Prosecutor Archibald Cox, "had little or nothing to do with Watergate."

5
The Legacy of the Weak Nixon Presidency

The tenure of Richard Nixon did not dangerously strengthen the Presidency. A more difficult question is whether it was dangerously weakened.

The riveting of national attention for a prolonged period on the subjects of presidential impeachment and presidential corruption can hardly escape having a pernicious effect on presidential power. It happened a century ago after Andrew Johnson and Ulysses Grant, when the Presidency was in danger of becoming little more, in Professor Woodrow Wilson's phrase, than "merely the executor of the sovereign legislative will."

Some now say that, with Nixon, there passed the modern American Presidency's place in the constitutional spectrum, its flexible powers, its tremendous prestige, and its commanding influence. "Now the institution of the Presidency," said the German newspaper *Die Welt*, reflecting a widely held view abroad, "is to be subordinated more strongly, perhaps much more strongly, to the influence of Congress." "The Presidency," summed up the *New York Post*, "has been sorely injured." Weakened by Nixon, said the *New York Times*. Weakened by the Congress, the courts, and the critics, said Nixon's supporters. "Now there are three ways to lose a President," Nixon aide Richard Moore was quoted as remarking with a touch of bitterness: "Death, impeachment, and pressure to resign—the newest amendment to the Constitution."

The newly installed President, Gerald Ford, promptly let it be known that he would share power more readily with Congress and the Cabinet. His unilateral approach to the Nixon pardon may be an indication that over the long haul he will not share very much. His unprecedented appearance before a House Judiciary Subcommittee to "discuss" the pardon (already granted without discussion) may be an indication of a more open approach; or it could signify an oversensitivity to Watergate-type criticism, suggesting the possibility that he is capable of voluntarily relinquishing authority necessary to an effective Presidency. Surely the speed with which Mr. Ford came under suspicion and attack, after a "honeymoon" of only one month, left him wondering whether the marriage had been consummated and left others wondering whether any President hereafter could succeed.

It is simply too early to know the long-range effect of these turbulent events of the past few years on legitimate presidential power. This country has equably survived the assassinations and otherwise distressful exits of several Presidents. It was clearly able to take Nixon's departure in stride, whatever it meant for the Presidency. But if the price of either his reign or his resignation is a loss of necessary presidential effectiveness, or a long series of either super-passive or one-term Presidents, or a permanent wound to the unique ability of that office to earn public confidence, then the permanent harm to our system could be greater even than that inflicted at Watergate.

The Effect of the Nixon Ouster

Nixon repeatedly warned those investigating him that they, not he, risked such great harm. The Office of the Presidency would be seriously damaged if forced to release tapes to the courts, grand jury, and Special Prosecutor, he said. The "frivolous" use of the impeachment process against him would set a precedent for the harassment of future Chief Executives. Resignation "would make it more difficult for future Presidents to make tough decisions." His compliance with House Judiciary Committee subpoenas, he wrote Chairman Rodino, would "render the executive branch henceforth and forever subservient to the legislative branch and . . . thereby destroy the Constitutional balance."

Earlier he had said:

A resignation or impeachment would weaken the Presidency . . . every President in the future . . . would be afraid to make unpopular decisions.

His attorneys warned the Supreme Court in their brief that an adverse decision—upholding the lower court's order that presidential tapes be produced, permitting his own Special Prosecutor to sue him, and letting stand the grand jury's finding that the President was a co-conspirator—would be disastrous for our system. The Presidency "will survive," they cautioned, but in a form significantly weaker than "the office contemplated by the framers and occupied by Presidents from George Washington through today."

If history should literally take Nixon at his word in his

speech of resignation—a speech that, while admirably temperate in tone, lacked any reference to the case against him—if it should thus conclude that he had in fact left office because, in his words, he no longer had "a strong enough political base in the Congress," then a dangerously destabilizing precedent would indeed have been set. Future Presidents might be expected to resign if the opposition party obtained enough seats to make both Houses safely veto-proof, or if key presidential proposals were voted down. Similarly, had Nixon been forced out months or even weeks earlier by the Democratic opposition without sufficient hard evidence, that also might have harmed the constitutional balance. Finally, there are those who fear that Nixon's pardon before trial clouds the question of his guilt and thus the propriety of the pressures that forced him out.

But in fact, as I trust history will recognize, his resignation came late enough to leave no doubt in the minds of overwhelming majorities in both houses of Congress and the country that his complicity in clearly impeachable offenses was well established. While the record would have been even stronger had Congress completed the impeachment and conviction process, the House by a vote of 412 to 3 did accept the unanimous and massively documented recommendation of its Judiciary Committee that President Richard Nixon should have been impeached, convicted, and ousted.

Despite a substantial public furor throughout the preceding year, with a majority turned against the President in public opinion polls, Congress did not rush to oust him. The impeachment proceedings, once begun, were painstakingly slow, careful, and rarely partisan. The members of the House Judiciary Committee, displaying a degree of courage, industry, and statesmanship that astonished even their friends in the House, were cautious in their judgments, thorough in their review of the evidence, and precise in their wording and rewording of the final Articles of Impeachment. Proceeding largely by consensus, they permitted the President's counsel to participate and call witnesses. Comparatively trivial or unsettled issues, unintentional or occasional lapses on Nixon's part, actions conceivably authorized only at the staff level, or actions subject to more than one interpretation, were omitted from the Articles approved against him. Only clear and repeated violations of his oath and statutory obligations were included.

Contrary to the charge by Vice President Ford that "a few crazies" were trying to undo the 1972 election, the final and most effective pressures inducing Nixon to resign came entirely from his own party and his own staff. He was not, emphasized the 10 Republicans on the House Judiciary Committee who finally turned against him, "hounded from office by his political opponents and media critics." He was, in Daniel Boorstin's important distinction, in violation of the *conscience* of the marketplace but never subjected to the lynch-law *judgment* of the marketplace. The climate of public concern compelled Congress to do its duty. But Nixon's popularity, his politics, his policies, his wisdom, his non-payment of taxes, even his character, were not the basis for either the impeachment hearings or the pressure to resign, nor was the difficult state of the economy or the world or his own party. The final transcripts that guaranteed his undoing revealed irrefutable evidence of serious felonies, and the revelations which subsequently emerged at the trial of his aides confirmed his personal guilt and involvement. Nor was he forced out for conduct characteristic of previous Presidents. Some of them committed grievous errors, but not high crimes and misdemeanors.

Nixon himself observed that he had seen "the Constitutional process through to its conclusion," that "the Constitutional purpose has been served" and that the matter need not be prolonged. His subsequent pardon for any federal crimes committed was not a condonation; it did not cover the noncriminal offenses for which his impeachment was also recommended by the committee; and his eager acceptance of that pardon for criminal offenses can only strengthen the verdict of history that he was guilty.

Thus presidential impeachment was responsibly attempted for the first time and it worked. This precedent, unlike the Andrew Johnson precedent, was a sound one for the future: broad enough to remain a deterrent, and narrow enough not to justify arbitrary pressures; broader than the "major federal criminal acts" theory advanced by Nixon's lawyers, but narrower than the "whatever a majority of the House considers an impeachable offense to be at a given moment" theory advanced in 1970 by Congressman Gerald Ford in seeking an impeachment of Justice William O. Douglas.

Resignation (already contemplated by the Constitution, notwithstanding Mr. Moore's observation) was in this instance—where the facts and guilt were clear—an acceptable means of shortening an inevitable process. There is no reason to fear that wrongdoing in the White House will hereafter be immune, or that either impeachment or forced resignations will be loosely sought against future Presidents any more than they have in the past century. The Nixon pardon may suggest to some future criminal in the Oval Office that by resigning before impeachment he can obtain immunity from indictment. But the storm raised by that pardon should cause him to doubt its effect as precedent.

Nor is there reason to fear that future Presidents and their confidential records and conversations will be subject to what Nixon called "unlimited search and seizure" fishing expeditions by Congress and the courts. Such expeditions should be prevented. I can well imagine the stultifying effect on many an Oval Office and Cabinet Room conversation in which I participated if those present had assumed their private advice to the President would be spread on the public record. It was difficult enough to get some presidential subordinates to speak up with dissenting or unorthodox views without further inhibiting their courage or causing them to weigh the political and public relations impact of their every sentence. But the House Judiciary Committee's conclusion that executive privilege could not be the subject of *impeachment* proceedings, and the Supreme Court's determination that such a privilege must defer to *criminal* proceedings, certainly should not deter candor among presidential advisers on controversial but legitimate government matters or prevent necessary and appropriate confidences in foreign affairs. On the contrary, the Supreme Court accorded the privilege doctrine a firmer judicial and constitutional basis than it had previously enjoyed; and a future President's specific invocation of the Fifth Amendment in an impeachment or other proceeding has not been ruled out.

Finally, the Supreme Court's agreement that the President could be sued by the Special Prosecutor, far from opening the floodgates, was based on a recognition of the latter's "unique authority and tenure" and "explicit power" to bring suit under the regulations establishing that office. That is not a precedent for future judicial control of executive operations.

In short, it is my conclusion as a lawyer who supports the Presidency that the disposition of the Nixon case by Congress, the courts, and the Special Prosecutor was just and proper as a precedent for the future, and should not make a strong Presidency impossible hereafter. The office was disgraced by its occupant, but it was not permanently injured by his co-equals in government. On the contrary, it was saved.

The Danger of an Impotent Presidency

That is fortunate. For the weak Nixon Presidency, masquerading as a strong and powerful Presidency, obscured the fact that this country today requires strong presidential leadership. Not unaccountable leadership, not a monopoly on leadership, but strong leadership nevertheless. Our only nationally elected executive must possess the flexibility and strength necessary to provide this country with responsible direction. We have survived caretaker Presidents in the past, but the price of those deceptively quiet periods in our history has always had to be paid later.

It is not altogether bad and certainly not coincidental that
the flow of power to the Presidency has accelerated at times of
major international crisis. Within his lawful authority, the
Executive—and only the Executive—can move with the
speed, energy and flexibility such crises usually require. Now
the problems we face are global, affecting all peoples: the
critical shortages of food, fertilizer, fuel, and certain other
basic commodities; the twin failures of arms control and
population control; the spread of world-wide inflation and the
spectre of world-wide depression. Within the last two years the
leaders of virtually every major democracy on earth found
themselves replaced or in political trouble because of their
inability to cope effectively with these and other problems. I
would not go as far as Senator J. William Fulbright (of all
people) went in the 1961 Stevens Memorial Lecture at
Cornell, when he argued:

that the price of democratic survival in a world of aggressive
totalitarianism is to give up some of the democratic luxuries of
the past . . . [through] the conferral of greatly increased
authority on the President.

But the present critical hour of mounting crises and leadership
vacuum is a most unlikely time to seek a passive or powerless
President in the most powerful nation on earth.

Nor was it coincidental that the other quantum leap in
permanent presidential power was spurred by the Great
Depression. A single point of responsibility, speaking for the
whole people, representing in egalitarian fashion the interests
of the powerless as well as the powerful, was indispensable in

the 1930s to pull this country through spiritually as well as economically.

Now our economic crisis again requires someone willing to make tough, unpleasant, and unprecedented decisions. Solutions to the problems of unemployment and laggard economic growth were never easy. But they were child's play in comparison with the search for politically acceptable and effective answers to our current problems—inflation in the midst of recession, quadrupled energy prices, a series of shortages—answers that are also consistent with our democratic framework, our global responsibilities, and our simultaneous need to reduce poverty and racial discrimination.

The President may in fact have *too little* power today to tackle fast-changing economic problems effectively. He cannot adjust taxes or spending without long congressional debate and approval, and by then it is often too late to apply a slow-acting fiscal stimulus or brake. He cannot openly control the Federal Reserve Board's policies on money and credit. He cannot veto excessive items in an appropriations bill or (as of this writing, with some cases still pending) impound the funds authorized thereunder. His powers over exports, imports, stockpiles, prices, wages, housing, debt, and government employment are all strictly limited by Congress and by the willingness of the bureaucracy to accept and implement his policies. He has few facilities for effective, long-range economic planning. He has no power to put into one enforceable package a "social contract" on taxes, wages, prices, interest rates, and spending that could enlist the support of all elements of the economy—as distinguished from merely holding an economic summit meeting.

A dozen years ago President Kennedy pointed out that he and Prime Minister Macmillan both sought the fiscal stimulus of a tax cut at about the same time. Macmillan's was enacted in six weeks. Kennedy's was still pending months later at his death.

Even the *New York Times*, recently in the forefront of those favoring a dispersal of White House powers, advised President Ford, with regard to inflation:

Successful prosecution of the job will require vigorous Presidential command of his own department and agency heads (who too often behave like interest-group representatives and spokesmen, rather than as servants of all the people).[1]

Unfortunately only editorial writers can enjoy the luxury of calling for more "vigorous Presidential command" of the executive branch one day and a more rapid dispersal of presidential power the next. There is no doubt that any increase in presidential discretion to meet the increased complexity and pace of our economic problems would involve an increased risk. There is always risk in giving any official any power. But there is also risk in denying ourselves the machinery to master our economic problems.

By definition, inclination, and long training, Congress cannot provide executive leadership. An issue such as the 1973 Middle East oil embargo produced separate legislative hearings in 40 separate committees, several inconsistent "emergency" bills to cope with the embargo—some not enacted until months after the embargo was ended—frequent statements of goals that had no prospect of fulfillment, and little in the way of meaningful congressional policy initiatives or in-depth research. Even while loudly protesting the practice of impoundment in late 1972, both houses passed bills leaving it to the President to decide which programs beyond his arbitrary budget ceiling would be cut.[2]

While the role of Congress should be strengthened to restore constitutional balance, that cannot be accomplished by weakening the Executive. Pennsylvania Avenue, it has been rightly said, is not a see-saw.

Nixon's abuse of the power to grant clemency, or to hire and fire employees, or to set milk support prices—to cite only three minor examples from the Watergate annals—does not mean that those powers could be better exercised by Congress. When the legislative branch tried to run the executive branch after the Andrew Johnson–Ulysses Grant era, it was not a period of greatness in Washington.

Those liberals, soured by Vietnam and Nixon, who desire a transfer of authority from the Presidency to Congress, appear to be acting on the basis of one or more assumptions—that most members of Congress are consistently less "hawkish" than the President on matters of war and peace, or less subject to the influence of the military-industrial complex, or more liberal on civil rights and civil liberties, or less responsive to the pressures of special-interest elites and short-term politics, or more ethical, open, nonpartisan, credible, and pure in deed and motivation. The overall record does not support a single one of those assumptions.

Nor can a collective legislative body, any more than a weak and passive President, convey the sense of dedication needed to redirect our energies and restore our sense of discipline and worth, and thus end our national crisis of the spirit, as Franklin Roosevelt did in 1933.

The single largest difficulty with curbing executive authority is that the power to do great harm is also the power to do great good.

• To have denied, as some would deny, any "implied constitutional authority" in the Presidency might have blocked some of Nixon's wiretaps; but such an approach would also have blocked Kennedy's first Executive Order in which, without express statutory authority, he expanded the surplus food distribution program for the poor, using funds from Customs reserves.

• To have eliminated, as some would eliminate, all secrecy in presidential foreign affairs operations unrelated to troop movements and intelligence sources might have prevented not only Nixon's bombing of Cambodia, but also his opening of relations with China.

• To have required, as some would require, advance congressional approval of any Executive Order which resembled legislative rule-making might have stopped both the Huston covert intelligence program and certain LBJ civil rights directives on housing and employment.

• Permitting the effectuation of no international agreements or understandings other than those submitted to the Senate, as recently proposed, might have blocked not only dubious deals with South Vietnam, but also the resolution of the Cuban missile crisis.

• A recently suggested constitutional or statutory amendment might have made possible a new presidential election when a firestorm of protest greeted Nixon's firing of Archibald Cox; but, under such an amendment, Truman might have lost his post for firing Douglas MacArthur.

• Had there been no White House Special Projects Fund providing every President since 1956 with $1.5 million for contingencies (and Congress has recently considered its abolition), Nixon would have had to look elsewhere to finance some of the plumbers' activities, but Kennedy would have been unable to establish in the face of an unconcerned Congress an emergency guidance counselor program to ease youth unemployment in the summer of 1962.

We cannot endlessly add to the powers of the Presidency with a Lincoln in mind without increasing a Nixon's opportunity to do harm. But we cannot unduly weaken the office with a Nixon in mind without hampering a law-abiding President's power to do good.

Proposed Structural Changes

With the aforementioned parallels in mind, I see no merit in the various structural and institutional changes in presidential power arrangements proposed or revived as suggested statutes or constitutional amendments in the wake of the Nixon Presidency. Most are Maginot lines designed to fight the last "war," the last crisis to confront the country, Watergate, without any thought as to their effect on the next one. These proposals will be only briefly mentioned here.

Some are merely gimmicks substituting ill-considered action for thought, thrown onto the floor in response to the cry of "do something." Those voiced to me, not all seriously, range from the perennial suggestion of a national ombudsman with no power base in the system, to an unworkably rigid apparatus for greater Cabinet participation, to novelties such as prohibiting public relations men in political campaigns or having the President periodically travel about listening in disguise like the ancient caliphs of Baghdad.

More serious is the regularly recycled proposal of a single six-year presidential term. Providing too long a tenure for an incompetent President and too short a tenure for a good one, this undemocratic step proposed with the best of intentions by Senator Mike Mansfield and others would remove every President from political accountability on the day he took office, freeing him from all concern about submitting his activities to the electorate. At least today a President is not placed in that position until the voters have had four years in which to judge his performance and precedents. Its advocates say they do not want the President to be influenced by political considerations. I do.

Such thoughtful observers as Michael Novak would have us imitate those countries which separate the head of state from the head of government, enabling our President as latter to avoid both the burden and the glory that come with ceremonial duties. I want to see less pomp and grandeur surrounding our Presidents. But neither our traditions, our politics, nor our concepts of efficiency neatly divide the head of state and head of government functions. The President would still need to dine with foreign leaders. He would still want to meet the 4-H Club chairmen whose parents are voters. He would still be revered for his power, even if a head of state lived in the White House and gave out the medals. And in the light of justifiable concern over every President's isolation, we should not now cut back on the speech-making, delegation-greeting, and dam-dedicating that may keep him at least in some slight contact with the citizenry. It is a mistake to exaggerate the amount of time wasted by Presidents in needless ceremonial functions that they have no wish to attend.

This is only one of many proposals borrowed from other systems of government, with no evidence that those systems have proven more successful than our own in stemming the flow of power to the executive. The parliamentary system, with merged legislative and executive power, and all members of Parliament including the Prime Minister and other ministers standing for office simultaneously, appears to have worked best in smaller, less diverse countries than ours—countries where the states are creatures of the national government, centralized national parties can discipline errant legislators, and senior civil servants dominate the ministries. None of these conditions applies here or is likely to be adopted here. Nor do all proponents of our accepting such a system realize the extent, under most parliamentary systems, to which a Prime Minister is becoming more and more a chief executive with centralized powers and can generally dominate Parliament for legislative purposes more readily than many an American President can dominate Congress.

In this country, the power to bring the executive branch down with a legislative vote of "no confidence" would introduce utter confusion. Many congressmen, fearful of the cost of campaigning, would not support such a motion when merited. But many with safe seats who are about to seek reelection anyway would support it regardless of merit; and given the recently volatile nature of the electorate's emotions and pressures, Presidents might be shuffled in and out before they could rearrange the furniture in the Green Room. At the very least, every President would be forced, far more than at present, to gratify the demands of a variety of special factions, cliques, and pork barrel interests.

The proposal that the President or department heads appear before a televised session of the full Congress or one house for questioning is also borrowed from parliamentary systems too unlike ours to make imitation valid. It might not hurt but it wouldn't help. The House Ways and Means Committee grilling the Secretary of the Treasury on tax policy—unless it is wholly his captive, which is rare—can gain far more of value than a session of 435 or 535 or 100 legislators questioning the President. Even the House Judiciary Committee questioning of President Ford on his pardon of Nixon elicited little of interest. Televising regular sessions are of value only if large numbers will watch; and however much the impeachment sessions of the House Judiciary Committee demonstrated that televised proceedings were not as speechy and empty as oft predicted, very few Cabinet quizzes offer sufficient drama or focus to outdraw "To Tell the Truth."

Like the vote of no confidence, other recent proposals are aimed at a quicker gratification of the public desire to get rid of an unpopular President: special elections, recall elections, or a less rigid standard for impeachment. Without doubt our system is slower than many others in responding even to legitimate needs to change Chief Executives; and the ordeal of Richard Nixon struck many as unnecessarily prolonged and traumatic. Yet in the end it is clear that quicker ouster would have left questions of guilt unresolved and the country bitterly divided.

It is best that Presidents, like containers, not be too easily disposable. Some unpopular acts (like John Adams' refusal to go to war) may turn out to be in the long-run national interest; some serious mistakes (like the Bay of Pigs) may constitute the experience from which wisdom comes; and, in the absence of some extraordinary occurrence such as a dual vacancy in the Presidency and Vice Presidency,[3] fixed elections are a stabilizing tradition we should not quickly cast aside. As previously noted, tampering with the system conceived by the framers has not always been successful.

The final group of proposed structural curbs would, in various forms, pluralize presidential decision-making: require him to obtain the concurrence of an Executive Council, the Cabinet, or of Congress or its leaders; or divide his duties, with separate executives for foreign and domestic affairs, or for policy and administration; or substitute government by Cabinet or committee. "The only way to defuse the Presidency," wrote Barbara Tuchman, "is to divide the power and spread the responsibility."

But making the President less responsible is not an answer to irresponsible Presidents. Plural bodies can, after some delay and fragmentation, produce a legislative decision acceptable to the lowest common denominator. But they cannot produce the kind of executive leadership this nation's problems require.

No matter whom a President is formally required to consult, he can still informally meet with a "kitchen cabinet" of his own choosing. Adding another structural layer of advice can increase delay and indecisiveness, but rarely safety. Advice is cheap, but it can be expensive for the country. For it is the President, because he is the one held responsible if policies go wrong, who is likely to be more cautious. Advisers, as JFK observed, can always "move on to new advice." (The Joint Chiefs of Staff recommended new military initiatives to him, he said, "the way one man advises another one about whether he should marry a girl. He doesn't have to live with her.")

Moreover, foreign and domestic, or policy and administrative, burdens are less separable now than ever. There is no need to reopen the framers' deliberate decision that a single Executive is best.

None of these structural or institutional reorganizations would have prevented Watergate. All would provide corrective action, if at all, only after the fact—as our present system already does. None would solve the political and operational problems at the heart of the matter which are discussed in the chapters that follow. Many would carelessly curb or reshape an office that over the long haul has served us well.

Unfortunately these ill-considered if well-motivated proposals that would harm the Presidency are part of the Nixon legacy. "Support the Presidency" proclaimed the buttons his organized devotees distributed during the impeachment proceedings. Support the Presidency. I still do. He did not.

III
The Sinews of Accountability

By now my basic conclusion should be clear: instead of punishing or weakening the Presidency for the sins of Richard Nixon, its powers should be renewed but held accountable—more closely watched, more precisely defined, more carefully kept within constitutional bounds, and more clearly answerable to the electorate, Congress, and our other institutions.

This is hardly a unique view. "The problem is not power as such," John Gardner of Common Cause has stated; "The problem is power that cannot be held accountable." The growth of unaccountable presidential power led to the imperial Presidency, wrote Arthur Schlesinger, and he called not for new structural reductions of presidential power but for greater accountability. The same term—accountability—was frequently repeated in the House Judiciary Committee's final impeachment report, in a special March 1974 study for the Senate Watergate Committee by the National Academy of Public Administration, and in an earlier Senate speech on the Presidency by Senator Walter Mondale of Minnesota.

Periodic accountability of sorts is provided by our quadrennial presidential elections. But between elections, Clinton Rossiter wrote, Presidents—unlike Prime Ministers under the parliamentary system—do not feel "the kind of day-to-day, act-to-act accountability that compels . . . [them] to mind every important step." *Ultimate accountability* is provided by the impeachment process. That is no longer the "mere scarecrow" that Thomas Jefferson had feared it would be, but, like all ultimate sanctions, it cannot and should not be used except in the most extreme circumstances. What we need is a routine system of *daily accountability* for Presidents, short of impeachment and between elections. This is not primarily a matter of statutes. But neither can we rely wholly on the greater national vigilance resulting from Watergate or on exhorting future Presidents to be "good." In addition to our written Constitution (which needs no change as a result of Watergate), our system like the British constitutional system rests on a body of accepted practices. It is certain of these practices—by Congress, the courts, and the American public—which now need to be changed if greater presidential accountability is to be achieved.

6
Making the President
More Accountable to Congress

An improvement in presidential accountability must begin where the framers began in Article I of the Constitution—with Congress. That body has too often delegated to the President unbridled authority or acquiesced in his taking it. It has permitted him to exercise much of its constitutional power over spending and to frustrate much of its power to oversee executive departments. It has enacted, as Senator Howard Baker has pointed out, hundreds of statutes ending with the vulnerable little phrase, "as the Secretary (or President) may direct."

With a frequent willingness to avoid tough issues by placing the whole burden of problem-solving on the Presidency, with no effective party discipline, with an excess of committees and subcommittees hamstrung by overlapping jurisdictions and unyielding chairmen, with proliferating professional staffs weakened by patronage and high turnover, with archaic rules that enable small minorities to block majority decisions and enable each member to blame someone else for a bill's failure, Congress has simply lacked the will, the machinery, and the resources to fight for its own constitutional role. Aware of its own failings regarding secrecy, ethics, and campaign finances, it has been reluctant to check the excesses of the Executive—at least until well after the fact.

Its acquiescence to presidential aggrandizements of power in foreign affairs has been particularly sorry. It has permitted the President to assume or circumvent its constitutional powers to authorize war and to consent to treaties. The concealment of the secret war in Cambodia obviously cannot be blamed on the Congress. But the members of the House Judiciary Committee, as mentioned, excluded this from the list of impeachable offenses in view of Congress's long-standing submission to Executive initiative in Indochina. Congress first gave the Executive a virtual blank check in the Gulf of Tonkin Resolution; then approved all fund requests; then defeated all meaningful attempts to condition appropriations; then enacted some toothless resolutions without force of law; and finally passed as a curb against future presidential war-making the supposedly bold new War Powers Act, which actually expanded the President's discretion beyond his constitutional grant and weakly exempted Indochina.

Nevertheless much of the criticism of Congress proceeds from the wrong premise, disparaging it in effect for not being more like a President: more efficient, unified, secretive, and decisive. Congress, according to some critics, should participate in deciding which specific CIA operations should proceed, or which applications for export credit to the Soviet Union should be approved. It should issue its own State of the Union message, says Senator Jacob Javits. It should have a veto power over executive agreements, says Senator Sam Ervin.

But Congress should be rebuked for failing in its legislative role, not for its deficiencies as an executive. Congress's job is not to run the country but to educate it, not to conduct the government but to finance, guide, and restrain it, not to make executive decisions but to make legislative rules. It can oversee and advise but not administer. Its task is not to keep secrets in but to get information out.

The trouble with Congress is not that so many important issues are debated at length, but that so few are. Too often the legislative debate on crucial military or foreign policy alternatives is perfunctory. Too often the debate on major national choices is left to inner White House councils. Too often congressional committees play at being special prosecutor instead of using their hearings to illuminate crucial national problems. Too many legislators are spread too thinly among too many subcommittees and other obligations. Too much time is given over to constituent errands, local projects, private bills, petty feuds, and reelection politicking.

Similarly, congressional leaders are often faulted for lacking presidential command, charisma, and decisiveness. Yet those leaders are the compromise choices of coalition party legislators who are not seeking presidential attributes in those posts. They are called leaders not because they are executives but because they are masters of the legislative process. They cannot except on rare occasions speak for all the members of Congress, nor should they. Their attendance at summit meetings abroad with the President or Secretary of State would be desirable more often than they are invited; but they should go as observers and advisers for the legislative branch, not as negotiators for the government.

To fulfill its legislative role, Congress must not always disapprove the President's proposals; but it must always hold him accountable—not merely on side issues and details, not merely in brief skirmishes, but in a sustained examination of all principal policy questions, including foreign affairs. "I have upheld all our Presidents when they spoke for my country to the world," President Ford told Congress; "I believe the Constitution commands this." Even if Mr. Ford as Congressman has supported the foreign policy of all Presidents, which is not the way I remember it, the Constitution commands no such thing. It contemplates debate and dissent on all issues, including foreign affairs, and both Congress and President Ford had best accustom themselves to that fact.

A new legislative monopoly of power is no answer to Nixon's attempted executive monopoly of power. An obstructionist Congress is not an improvement over a defiant President. Nor should Congress ever push the President as far as it theoretically could—by cutting off all White House Staff appropriations except for a part-time stenographer, for example, or refusing all Cabinet confirmations. While making provision for conflict by means of its system of checks and balances, the Constitution also presupposes comity and collaboration between the separate branches of government. It assumed a mutual respect for each other's rights and roles, a common undertaking to make the system work.

American schoolchildren are taught our federal system with an emphasis on separated, not shared, power. But Judge Sirica in the first Nixon tapes case recalled these words of John Marshall:

While the Constitution *diffuses* power, the better to secure liberty, it also contemplates that practice will *integrate* the dispersed powers into a workable government. It enjoins upon its branches separateness but *interdependence*, autonomy but *reciprocity*.[1]

Nixon unsurprisingly took another view. "The moment that a President is looking over his shoulder down to Capitol Hill before he makes a decision," said our thirty-seventh Chief Executive, "he will then be a weak President." In his transcribed conversations with John Dean, he termed Congress "irrelevant . . . irresponsible . . . so enormously frustrated they are exhausted." But the truly strong Presidents have all recognized the benefit to them of consulting and compromising with Congress. A constructive partnership will allow and indeed foster a certain undefined amount of presidential initiative, executive privilege, temporary impoundments, and executive agreements with foreign countries. A posture of mutual contempt can only invite specific and rigid legislative restrictions.

President Ford's willingness to appear before a congressional committee investigating the Nixon pardon was a skillful step toward comity and accountability. It made clear that the excessive Nixon doctrine of executive privilege had been discarded, and did so without setting a binding precedent that could cause Mr. Ford or his successors to be harassed and demeaned in the future. Not surprisingly, most Committee members were too deferential to probe as deeply into the pardon, and the related agreement on tapes, as the controversy deserved.

Collaboration and comity, however, do not wholly exclude combat, particularly if the executive and legislative are sharply divided ideologically. Herbert Hoover's stiff nonpolitical passivity toward the Depression Congress produced little more than the disastrous Smoot-Hawley tariff and the infant Reconstruction Finance Corporation. In contrast, Harry Truman's peppery battles with the Republican Eightieth Congress produced an outpouring of major legislative landmarks. Hamilton's concept of "power as the rival of power" must work both ways. Combat, however, should not be confused with contempt. Battles should be fought over major issues of substance, not personalities or prerogatives.

Increasing accountability is not primarily a matter of procedural change. The new Budget and Impoundment Control Act[2] is intended to require Congress to coordinate all its multiple actions having an effect on revenues and spending, assisted by an expert Budget Office of its own. While it could in time become merely a new device for entrenched interests to block appropriations for social progress, this Act should, if properly used with sufficient discipline, substantially help the legislative branch regain its constitutional direction of revenues and spending, the real keys to the kingdom. But how many other procedural changes would actually enhance its ability to stand up to the President? The legislative reforms of one generation or faction are often viewed as regression by another—limiting the influence of the party caucus, or transferring power from the Speaker to committee chairmen, or realigning committee jurisdictions, or limiting floor amendments.

For example, the seniority system has undoubtedly produced more than a few aged and arbitrary committee and subcommittee chairmen with the ability to defeat, delay, or dilute legislation desired by a majority. The age of the average committee chairman exceeds the limit set in most corporate compulsory retirement plans. But some of the seniority system's traditional critics may lapse into silence in the next few years as it produces, particularly in the Senate, an overwhelming majority of liberal chairmen. Modification may still be in order. But the proposal to merely throw each committee chairmanship open to an annual vote by its members or by the party caucus would invite undesirable log-rolling and lobbying. Just as President Grant got rid of Charles Sumner as Chairman of the Senate Foreign Relations Committee, future Presidents—operating the most resourceful lobby in Washington—might too easily impose their choice of chairmen.

To hold the Executive accountable, Congress should enact an improved War Powers Act prohibiting any presidential usurpation of this power in the absence of a genuine emergency, not merely limiting such usurpation to 90 days. It should also enact certain statutory safeguards mentioned below. But the recovery of its role in holding presidential power accountable is not primarily dependent upon new constitutional or statutory amendments. Congress does not need more "power." Instead it needs above all else the will—"the guts"—to use more effectively the machinery and powers it already possesses.

Confirming the Cabinet

Consider, for example, the Senate's power to confirm the appointment of officials nominated by the President.

I do not join with those who criticize any presidential "interference" in the executive branch, or who deny that this collection of agencies created by Congress is his to direct. The modern President could not meet his responsibilities if foreclosed from welding a coherent and consistent approach to national problems among the executive departments.

Nevertheless, the modern Cabinet provides far less of an institutional check on presidential power than it might. Nor is executive accountability aided by the increasing transfer of operating responsibilities from department heads—who are accountable to Congress—to White House staff members, who are not.

Every President is tempted, particularly in foreign affairs, to bother less with the differing views of allies, congressmen, and Cabinet members by bringing the maximum number of government levers into his immediate White House orbit. Wilson found it more agreeable to rely on Colonel House than on Secretary of State Lansing. Franklin Roosevelt looked more to Harry Hopkins than to Cordell Hull. Kennedy looked more to White House aide McGeorge Bundy than to Secretary of State Dean Rusk, and to a greater extent than any predecessor refused to regard the Cabinet collectively as a consultative body.

Nixon went further. Even as he espoused the decentralization of power, he centralized it in the White House as never before. He preceded his first term by glorifying the importance of all his Cabinet members in a television extravaganza. He preceded his second term by demanding that they all submit their resignations.

During that first term he excluded Secretary of State William Rogers from major foreign policy deliberations, tried to bypass Secretary of Defense Melvin Laird, cursed out Attorney General Richard Kleindienst for having the gall to raise a legal question, and had as little as possible to do with Secretary of the Interior Walter Hickel, Secretary of Housing and Urban Development George Romney, and other domestic department heads. Virtually all departments were run by the White House staff. "When he says 'jump!'" observed John Ehrlichman of the relationship between Nixon and his appointees, "they only ask 'how high?'"

The Senate confirmed the largely nameless, faceless men who in time comprised the bulk of Nixon appointees—capable men in most instances but too lacking in political independence to resist presidential excess, too passive or unsophisticated to question any White House aide who invoked the President's name, and too little known to achieve anything by resigning in protest.

With rare exception, the Cabinet confirmation process has been lightly regarded by both the Senate and the White House. Presidents are properly entitled to wide discretion in choosing the members of their teams. Assuming that no financial conflict of interest exists, a nominee's philosophy and competence are usually examined only superficially. No Senator can know with certainty how the nominee will conduct himself in the future; and every nominee solemnly promises to consult with the Congress and to be a credit to his parents and country

But the Senate at that moment has virtually its only chance

to assure itself of that Cabinet member's ability to keep watch on the President and share in his power. This was demonstrated in the ability of the Senate Judiciary Committee to extract from Attorney General–designate Elliot Richardson a fateful pledge on the independence of the Special Prosecutor. The analogous vice-presidential confirmation hearings opened Gerald Ford's eyes on civil rights and Nelson Rockefeller's on improper gifts, or so they both have said.

As Senator Mondale remarked of Cabinet confirmation hearings:

It is the one chance we have to come to know [Cabinet members]. And it is the last time they are kind to us.

The Senate should take a closer look more often.

* If mediocrities too weak to play a watchdog role or to manage their departments or to threaten resignation are being nominated in order to facilitate the monopolization of White House power, then they need not be confirmed by the Senate.

* If a nominee lacks the sensitivity to distinguish between the public interest and the President's interests, or is not tough enough to insist upon a voice in the selection of his own subordinates and policies, or cannot guarantee to accept all congressional invitations to testify and produce appropriate documents, or is (as some of Governor Rockefeller's appointees were) not only politically but financially dependent upon his chief, then that nominee need not be confirmed.

* If a prospective Secretary of State cannot reach a harmonious accommodation with the Senate Foreign Rela-

tions Committee on when executive agreements will be used instead of treaties and when the Congress will be informed of their negotiation, then he need not be confirmed.

• If any prospective department head is not willing to forego the role of presidential counselor held by Lewis Strauss, Henry Kissinger, and George Shultz, or is not willing to pledge to stay at least the two years necessary to speak from strength in his job, or has not been the subject of advance senatorial advice as well as consent, then he need not be confirmed.

I am not suggesting that the Senate prevent the executive branch from speaking with a single voice on policy, the budget, and other matters. Nor can any specified number of Cabinet meetings—even though in my experience they can have some limited role in improving communications and rapport—be mandated by the Senate, at least not without making most of them useless farces in which no confidential or important matters are discussed. But by insisting upon the nomination of strong and influential department heads, without interfering with the President's right to choose men and women who share his philosophy, the Senate could enhance the Cabinet's role as an insurer of presidential accountability.

Presidents might grumble, but over the long run such a policy could only help them as well, encouraging more dedicated and talented individuals to accept Cabinet appointment. By placing men and women of substance in all of the top administrative positions, delegating authority to them, and encouraging them to take initiative and make decisions within the broad policy framework he establishes, a President can greatly increase his effectiveness.

That is something that Nixon, despite his support of a sweeping reorganization plan that would on paper have strengthened the surviving departments, never seemed to understand. The earliest American Cabinets included noted statesmen, party leaders, presidential rivals, and other possessors of independent power. But I wonder if anyone, including Nixon himself, can recall the names of all the members of his final Cabinet.

Mediocrities in anyone's Cabinet are likely to be taken over by their departments' specialized experts and constituencies. They are soon viewed by the White House as representing outside pressure groups to the President instead of vice versa. In contrast, top-flight Cabinet members, who feel they have some voice in administration policy-making and some flexibility in defending and administering it, can work for the President's interests with the bureaucracy and Congress far more effectively than can White House aides. (Quality Cabinet members and quality White House aides can even work harmoniously together, if each respects the other's role. Henry Stimson, for example, unlike Cordell Hull, regarded Harry Hopkins as a "Godsend.") Should any Cabinet appointee turn out to be less than his reputation (as is often the case) or too prone to serve narrow departmental constituencies, then the President should change Cabinet members instead of keeping the wrong man in office while transferring his decision-making functions into the White House.

Watergate has prompted renewed suggestions that politicians be kept out of the Cabinet. Clearly, political fund-raising activities should terminate upon appointment to federal office. But it would be desirable to have more politicians in the Cabinet—more men and women with their own political base who will feel more secure, more willing to speak up, more knowledgeable of congressional prerogatives, and better able to take their case to the country if the President goes too far. The public will notice the resignation in protest of a William Jennings Bryan or an Elliot Richardson. Indeed, even presidential appointees without political constituencies of their own will be heard (as Jerry ter Horst demonstrated), if they have enough independence and integrity to resign on a question of conscience. But in this country that noble route is rarely taken.

Pruning White House Staff Functions

Several Senators have recently suggested that all senior White House aides should also be made subject to Senate confirmation (and, a logical concomitant, subject to requests to testify before congressional committees). It is understandable that Senators wish they had known more about the qualifications and philosophy of the Nixon inner circle. To the extent that executive programs are actually administered out of the White House—as they were under Ehrlichman's Domestic Council and Kissinger's swollen "little State Department"—Congress cannot meet its own responsibilities, for then the real administrators are unavailable to Capitol Hill. As one Senator put it,

They let Rogers [as Secretary of State] handle Norway and Malagasy, and Kissinger would handle Russia and China and anything else he was interested in.

But subjecting immediate White House personnel to confirmation and testimony would be a mistake. It would institutionalize the practice of moving functions from the departments to the White House by removing a principal objection to that practice. It would also speed the disappearance of any distinction between two very different types of presidential appointees:

(1) those in the White House whose sole function is to render advice and assistance to the President—his personal choices who properly should not be subject to Senate confirmation, intimate advisers who under normal circumstances should not be asked to appear before congressional committees, political aides who are not expected to act as checks on presidential action; and

(2) those whose direct administrative and operating responsibilities and independent power (as distinct from supervisory duties) should not be in the White House in the first place. This includes any Cabinet member serving simultaneously as the White House aide who is supposed to weigh objectively for the President the conflicting views of various Cabinet members.

Instead of subjecting all senior White House advisers to confirmation, Congress through appropriations conditions or separate statute should get those operating officials in the second category and their functions out of the President's office; get them back into agencies created by Acts of Congress (or if necessary into the Executive Office); and then make those officials subject to the discipline and accountability of confirmation and testimony. In addition, Congress should require that the duties of each principal White House aide be made public, which would not only provide a safeguard against abuse but also encourage Presidents to limit their staffs to those performing clearly essential functions. Finally, the appropriations committees in their review of the White House budget should check any abuse of the President's right to bypass Civil Service regulations and any abuse of his right to borrow personnel from other agencies. Such review can also make certain that no "plumbers" unit and no operating functions are being newly established in the White House.

Once that is done, Congress should be wary of those renewed recommendations that it also strictly prescribe the structure of the White House professional staff. Like opposing generals who take care not to bomb each other's command headquarters, Congress and the President have traditionally and rightly been cautious about interfering with each other's legitimate needs for help.

It is true that the White House staff multiplied far too fast during Nixon's last four years; and too large a staff is not in the public interest, fragmenting policy instead of coordinating it, and discouraging creativity and competence in the departments instead of inspiring them.

It is also true that Congress is not often vigilant when providing funds for the White House staff. Nixon established on his own the Domestic Council, a huge operating agency not accountable to Congress through confirmation and testimony, whose payroll was used to launch the plumbers operation; yet

Congress kept giving him the money he asked for it. (One Senator complained in 1973 that he had never seen Ehrlichman's successor as head of the Council, Kenneth Cole. Cole was the most important man in government in domestic affairs, he said, but "I couldn't pick him out of a police line-up.")

Nevertheless, once the staff has been limited to personal presidential advisers and assistants as suggested above, the President should within reasonable limits be entitled to fill and organize those positions as he sees fit. Whether he is more comfortable with a staff system designed like a wheel or like a pyramid, with one superchief or with several senior aides, with a Jesuit speechwriter or an "Irish mafia," no law or appropriations limitations should force him to work in someone else's pattern. It is rare that one President's preference for staff organization resembles his predecessor's. It is equally rare that it even resembles his own of a few years earlier.

Outside the White House is that sprawling collection of special functions and units known as the Executive Office of the President. Some White Houses use the EOP as a farm league, some use it as a source of experts and implementers, and some use it as Elba.

The Office of Management and Budget (OMB), a powerful, White House oriented successor to the Bureau of the Budget in EOP, was the object of considerable complaint during the Nixon Administration. Yet there was nothing new or improper about its coordinating for the President policy and program development as well as formulation of the budget. No doubt its

Director and Deputy Director had a heavy hand as some department heads charged, and those Department heads should always have had a right of appeal from OMB decisions to the White House and ultimately to the President. Certainly, as operating officials, the OMB Director and his Deputy should have been subject to Senate confirmation, and more available to assist and inform the members and committees of Congress. But stripping OMB of its policy functions, and prohibiting it from seeking a unified administration approach throughout the executive branch, as urged by its critics on the Ford Transition Task Force, will surely inspire more chaos than departmental creativity, and may only result in a transfer of those functions out of OMB into a still larger White House staff.

Too many of the other Executive Office units are also operating agencies. They have been put there by Congress on the grounds that their functions—energy, the environment, and poverty, for example—overlap several departments. But there are few subjects in government that do not overlap several departments. Education, the environment, transportation, job training, job safety, food, and narcotics are typical examples. Placing operating functions in the Executive Office, if their officials are subject to Senate confirmation and congressional testimony, may be an acceptable compromise, and would be preferable to putting them directly in the White House. But a Congress (and President) intent on dispersing authority and strengthening the Cabinet could transfer many of these functions to existing departments and agencies whose executives are perfectly capable of coordinating them for everyone else. Their peers would complain, but White House staffs in part exist to hear such complaints.

Securing Information

Presidential accountability could also be increased dramatically without reducing legitimate presidential powers if Congress fully exercised its right to executive branch information. Unannounced presidential decisions based on unpublished information from undisclosed sources were at the heart of both Vietnam and Watergate.

Upon taking office, President Ford pledged "openness, candor and honesty," and backed this up by being photographed picking up the morning paper in his bathrobe. One month later he pardoned his predecessor, and gave him custody of potentially incriminating tapes, after secret preparations and negotiations for reasons only obscurely explained during his appearance before a House Judiciary subcommittee. He also vetoed a bill to strengthen the Freedom of Information Act and became the first President to proclaim the desirability of the CIA's clandestine activities.

The country should not have been shocked. All new Presidents make solemn vows of disclosure, but find secrecy a compulsive White House habit. (Ford's supporters said his would be an open Presidency, like Truman's. It should be recalled that Truman, for all his merit and candor, issued an Executive Order permitting every agency in government to classify information as "secret" and "top secret," empowered the CIA to undertake covert operations abroad, dispatched troops to Korea on his own authority, and promulgated a loyalty-security program for federal employees under which secret informants prospered.)

The nuclear age and cold war only accentuated a natural presidential instinct to conceal information from Congress. Secrecy adds to a President's aura of omniscience, shrouds his mistakes, protects his surprises, and deters his critics. Just as every White House fears Congress's power to block presidential efforts, every President prefers to dole out only that information that will help his cause.

Congress intermittently advances a number of slogans on this question along with statutes to embody the slogans: government in the sunshine, freedom of information, the people's right to know, open government. But it has opened comparatively little.

One reason is Congress's own secrecy. The House Democratic caucus in 1973 voted to require the opening of all committee sessions to the public *unless* a majority of members voted otherwise. (It later agreed to permit publication of votes taken in the caucus itself *if* a majority votes to do so.) The Senate has thus far refused to go that distance. Congress will have more credibility in demanding fuller executive branch disclosure when it removes the mote from its own eye.

Another reason is congressional deference to the same "national security" mystique invoked at Watergate. Many members of Congress do not want to receive classified information on foreign and military affairs or the responsibility that might accompany it. Others get it but do not think their less trustworthy colleagues or constituents should. Obviously, some nondisclosure is essential in foreign affairs. But the national security justification of secrecy has now been expanded far beyond all reason or necessity.

At last count over 17,000 government employees, some with a rank no higher than ensign, had the authority to stamp a secrecy classification on a government document. In the Kennedy White House I frequently read papers routinely stamped "top secret" without serious thought by the stamper as to what security interests would actually be compromised if Congress and the press had that data. Often the information was not secret from the nation's adversaries abroad, only from the President's adversaries in Congress. Often it was not secret at all, or was not secret for long, or consisted of information more likely to be embarrassing than harmful if released. It is not surprising that the declassification of some 50 million pages of secret documents, in the 17 months following the issuance in October 1972 of new guidelines, has had no noticeably adverse impact on the nation's security.

The greater danger to our national security interests lies in the excessive use of secrecy by the executive branch—by officials with an elitist, patronizing attitude toward Congress, or by Presidents who depend upon secrecy to manipulate congressional and public opinion and to prevent enlightened debate. A Senate subcommittee in 1974 counted 225 instances in the past 10 years, over 90 percent under Nixon, in which executive branch agencies refused to provide information requested by Congress on subjects ranging from the Kent State shootings to postmasters' salaries.[3]

A Congress that knows only what the Executive wants it to know is not an independent body. It cannot intelligently perform its legislative, educative, and oversight functions, hold the President accountable, or take steps to prevent, correct, or discontinue mistaken or wrongful actions.

If the Congress truly believes in open government, now is the time to open it up. Every committee should obtain from the agency it oversees, with minimum limitations, in usable form and without having to stumble onto the right questions, whatever that committee needs and requests—including classified intelligence and diplomatic reports, the decisions and activities of the departments, their private interest group contacts and rulings, and all the other administration policies, commitments, studies, alternatives, and factual developments that will help Congress know what the executive branch is doing. That is accountability.

It may not work. There will certainly be risks, errors, embarrassment, and some loss of executive effectiveness. Some important discussions may be inhibited. No one should assume that Congress will (or should) withhold from the press and public very much of the information it receives. Some heretofore sacrosanct subjects will be debated. But these are precisely what Congress and the country should be debating. Why not try it? Why not start erring on the side of overdisclosure instead of overconcealment?

This is not to suggest that there should be no secrets whatever. Candid advice to the President on government policies, like the internal deliberations of a court, should be privileged to assure candor. Ideas still in the fetal stage—

which, if prematurely disclosed, might be aborted by powerful interests—should be protected until birth. Confidential information obtained by government agencies—employee discipline records, medical reports, criminal and credit files, trade secrets, and tax returns, for example—should not be spread on the public record, nor should the traditionally private phases of adjudicative proceedings. Internal deliberations on monetary affairs, contracts, or other matters where an unfair advantage could be obtained by outside interests with access to them, should not be public.

In world affairs, vulnerable sources of essential foreign intelligence should not be compromised. Nor can we rely wholly on open covenants openly arrived at. Foreign governments should be assured of at least a degree of temporary secrecy in any of our military and diplomatic operations affecting them and at least a degree of temporary confidentiality in any sensitive deliberations in which they participate. I would not, for example, have subjected to public debate President Kennedy's advance discussions on what response he should make to the Russian missiles in Cuba or his exchange of messages with Nikita Khrushchev on that subject. But I would have willingly sent to Congress the conflicting reports he received on Vietnam and the conflicting studies on what should be done about it. How I wish we had!

A congressional insistence upon unprecedented disclosure and declassification would not injure the Presidency. Some of the most far-reaching decisions of Jefferson, Lincoln, and Franklin Roosevelt were openly announced and explained. Kennedy, having quickly abandoned a request he made after the Bay of Pigs for more media self-discipline, told the *New York Times* that he wished it had disregarded all advance warnings regarding the Bay of Pigs operation and published those plans before he mistakenly permitted them to proceed. For excessive concealment is not essential to a strong Executive. Manipulation through secrecy is not leadership. In time it blinds the President to reality, invites suspicion of his credibility, and places a greater blame upon him if his policy ultimately fails.

A strong President who could kick the secrecy habit might even discover that he liked open government. It will call for a greater exercise of his skills in leadership, education, and mobilization of support. It will be seen as good politics. A wider recognition of the stark facts and harsh choices with which he is confronted might win him greater understanding. Decisions taken after full discussion are likely to retain greater public support longer.

Opening the channels of communication to the Congress also unclogs them within the executive branch itself. More than one presidential misjudgment could have been prevented had the government's own experts only known about them in advance. Public discussion by Congress and commentators can also identify otherwise unnoticed defects or alternatives before a particular course is finally adopted.

Moreover, presenting sensitive information to Congress and the electorate in a coherent form is preferable from the President's viewpoint to partial and distorted leaks and rumors. Given the increasing number of multilateral foreign policy issues involving a wider number of countries and agencies, few U.S. positions on international matters stay wholly secret very long anyway.

Finally, a President who is properly dubious about the demand by a supposed ally that he conceal American military activity in that country—or the pressure from a powerful corporate supporter that he intervene in its antitrust or overseas nationalization disputes—could politely refuse by noting it would soon become public.

Some statutory changes would help. Congress has already passed over President Ford's veto a bill[4] to strengthen the 1966 Freedom of Information Act, which has been an incomplete success due to bureaucratic evasions, sweeping national security exemptions, and a lack of precise penalties, time limits, and criteria. Further laws are also needed to curb the discretion of those 17,000 document classifiers, to speed the process of declassification, and to specify congressionally authorized standards and penalties for serious violations of the classification laws (in contrast with a Nixon bill which would have imprisoned officials and newsmen for releasing harmless documents that had no business being classified).

A broader Government in the Sunshine Act—its name inspired by Justice Brandeis's famous comment (on publicizing social and industrial ills) that "sunshine is the best disinfectant"—could bring into the open certain civilian agency decision-making meetings, more congressional committee sessions, and most agency contacts with officials and private interests regarding public property, contracts, money, or policies. But, again, what is needed more than new statutes is a willingness by Congress to insist on that to which it is already entitled.

The benefits of this approach would not be exaggerated. The number of necessary exemptions will still be large, making uniform implementation difficult. "Informal" meetings in private will still be the occasion of many key decisions that will then be ratified by formal meetings in public. Connivers and conspirators in high places will still not voluntarily confess their illicit activities. Most declassified documents will turn out to have little of importance that was not already leaked, known, or surmised. Many members of Congress will still be too awed by the national security information provided them by authoritative witnesses from the executive branch to question the President's conclusions. Nevertheless a more open government would surely be a major step toward accountability that could simultaneously enhance public confidence.

Overseeing Surveillance

Reducing secrecy does not mean reducing privacy. The President and other ranking government officials necessarily sacrifice a portion of their right to privacy as it pertains to their official duties. But, with such exceptions as the President and his most glamorous appointees allow in order to please their press and fans, the personal lives of both public officials and private citizens, so long as they act within the law, are no one else's business.

Unfortunately, in order to ascertain compliance with the law, the government is in the business of inquiring into private lives, social relationships, personal habits, tax returns, protest activities, military service records, financial accounts, and the like. However necessary such investigative and surveillance activity may be—and much of it is not necessary—the existence of personnel, files, and facilities for these purposes in the executive branch presents any President with enormous temptation for abuse.

Nixon's misuse of the Federal Bureau of Investigation, Central Intelligence Agency, Secret Service, and Internal Revenue Service for partisan or personal ends, as well as the creation and use of his own "plumbers," indicates that reliance on presidential good faith and good judgment in this area is not enough. Nixon was engaged, said the House Judiciary Committee, in "authorizing and directing actions that violated or disregarded the rights of citizens and that corrupted . . . the lawful functioning of [these] executive agencies."

One immediate response was Senator Robert Byrd's call to make these surveillance agencies "independent." Independent of whom? Turning their confidential files over to Congress would not protect the privacy of American citizens. Freeing them from all political control—as J. Edgar Hoover might have liked—would not provide assurance of their responsiveness to the public will or their caution in private investigations. Even so-called independent agencies, experience teaches, can be subject to improper political interference.

Instead, the existing laws against bugging, eavesdropping, wire-tapping, mail covers, break-ins, and political surveillance, even in the name of national security, must be reviewed; if loopholes are found to exist, they must be closed. The creation of any new units for any of these purposes, in the White House or elsewhere, must be prohibited. The White House may legitimately request from the Internal Revenue Service statistical data for policy-making as well as information on the tax-paying status of prospective appointees. But Nixon's secret political investigation unit within the Internal Revenue Service was a dangerous use of the taxing power to curb unorthodoxy. Actual income tax returns must by statute be kept out of the White House and out of politics; and all White House or other requests to the IRS for information should be reported to Congress.

In addition, Congress must exercise more surveillance of these surveillance agencies. In the past, the subcommittees charged with overseeing the FBI and CIA, particularly in the Senate, have served more to shield them from criticism than to check their excesses. They have customarily provided more funds than requested and have asked few hostile questions. (The word "oversight" has two meanings, and they chose the wrong one.) If these subcommittees cannot do the job, more responsive congressional committees and outside review boards should be established and instructed.

Some legislators were said to fear J. Edgar Hoover for what use he might make of his secret files on them. (This is not new. Some 70 years earlier Theodore Roosevelt wanted the Secret Service authorized to investigate congressmen.) But such fears and such files are intolerable in a democracy.

The covert political and paramilitary operations of the CIA

(as distinct from its foreign intelligence collection and analysis functions) still occupy too much of its budget and personnel, and still contribute to a domestic climate that makes stealth and deception more acceptable. (Nor should any *domestic* activities of the CIA, including even intelligence gathering, have ever been permitted—for these are in violation of its charter.) The continuing value of these clandestine operations and their effect on U.S. foreign relations should be critically reexamined by Congress and the new blue-ribbon commission in the light of progress toward détente, developments in international and constitutional law, the new technology of intelligence collection and analysis, and the demonstrated ineffectiveness of any foreign operations, overt or covert, which are not backed by a broad national consensus. While a contingency capability may still be required for many years, the objective of most if not all covert activities truly justifiable in the name of national security could be accomplished with greater prospect of success and less risk by open, above-board means.

Finally, the Director of the FBI should report not to the White House but to the Attorney General, and report all, not some, of his agency's surveillance, counter-intelligence, and other activities. These activities in turn should be limited by precise congressional guidelines. The recently revealed COIN-TELPRO (Counter-Intelligence Program) effort under J. Edgar Hoover to infiltrate, disrupt, and incite a wide range of organizations, not all of them even extremist or violence prone, should never have been allowed to exist without legislative review.

If Congress can take all these steps, Watergate may yet prove to have had some positive effects.

Withdrawing Emergency Powers

The FBI's controversial role in gathering internal security intelligence is apparently based not on any direct congressional authorization, but on a series of ancient FDR executive orders and directives, some of them still secret. When Congress was given an opportunity to ratify this practice in 1940 in a Resolution drafted by the Justice Department, it preferred to dodge the issue and rely on President Roosevelt's invocation of emergency powers.

Only within the past year has Congress discovered the extent of all the emergency powers it had granted to the Presidency in the past century or more. Without realizing it, we have been living in a state of presidentially declared national emergency—several overlapping emergencies, in fact —since 1933. As a result, every President has possessed unlimited yet congressionally authorized power to institute martial law, detain civilians, and seize property, commodities, and all means of transportation, communication, and production. That kind of power should not have been given to a convocation of saints, much less Richard Nixon.

Nor is that all.

• When Congress in 1972 contemplated the elimination of funds for the Indochina War, the Nixon Administration was prepared to finance it under the 1861 emergency "Feed and

Forage Act," still on the books,[5] which allowed the Union Army in times of emergency to purchase clothing, food, fuel, and other supplies without congressional appropriation.

• When the Kennedy Administration in 1963 as part of its effort to isolate Cuba economically promulgated the Cuban Assets Control Regulations, they were based not on any legislative mandate on Cuba but on the 1950 Korean War proclamation of emergency, never terminated.[6]

• When Woodrow Wilson's 1917 bill authorizing the arming of American merchant ships was filibustered to death by a group of Senators, an old statute permitting the President to act on his own by invoking emergency powers was discovered by Assistant Secretary of the Navy Franklin Roosevelt.

Congress is now clearly determined to terminate these emergency powers and to prescribe more precise limits for their invocation and termination in the future. Unfortunately, the history of the Civil War, two World Wars, the Great Depression, the Korean War, and the Gulf of Tonkin Resolution indicates that general guidelines and warnings will be insufficient—that Congress has been willing when confronted with a crisis to acquiesce all too quickly to virtually any presidential request for, or mere presidential proclamations of, open-ended emergency powers.

The House in 1933 passed Roosevelt's emergency banking bill sight unseen after 38 minutes of debate, thereby affirming his emergency proclamation of three days earlier which drew in turn upon the World War I Trading With the Enemy Act. Both houses quickly and overwhelmingly passed Johnson's Gulf of Tonkin Resolution in 1964, before ascertaining what had happened on the night in question and without realizing that the text authorized full-scale war for several years. Even in the Watergate summer of 1974, the House Armed Services Committee after a 30-minute hearing voted to extend a Civil Defense statute under which a Nixon Executive Order would authorize any President who "anticipated" an attack on the United States to impose total controls on free expression, free enterprise, free labor, and free education.

To maintain presidential accountability, Congress must hereafter be far more cautious with its grants of discretion in exigent times. The alertness of the Congress in 1974, spurred by Senators Church and Mathias, to the need to circumscribe those powers is commendable. But a new general declaration of policy will not be enough if future Congresses respond to specific requests with the haste and open-ended grants that have characterized their predecessors.

This is not to deny the need for Congress to delegate certain emergency powers, or the need for instant presidential action, in that rare genuine exigency that does not allow time for customary legislative processes. But the history of legislative-executive relations on emergencies is nevertheless one more example of the consistent tendency of too many members of Congress to pay undue deference to the Presidency. Even when the President has been their former colleague on the Hill, as the last four have been, too many of the most hardened legislators genuflect when he says "national security," "national emergency," or "national interest." That is not accountability.

"I have no illusion," said Justice Robert Jackson in his concurring opinion in the *Steel Seizure* case:

that any decision by this Court can keep power in the hands of Congress if it is not wise and timely in meeting its problems . . . If not good law, there was worldly wisdom in the maxim attributed to Napoleon that "The tools belong to the man who can use them." . . . [O]nly Congress itself can prevent power from slipping through its fingers.[7]

7
Making the President
More Accountable to the Courts

When most Americans think of checks on unlawful exercises of governmental power, they think first of the courts. The supreme law of the land under Article VI of the Constitution *is* the Constitution; and under Article III the whole of judicial power, including the application and interpretation of the Constitution and other laws, is given to the judicial branch. From *Marbury* v. *Madison* in 1803 to *U.S.* v. *Nixon* in 1974, the courts have exercised the sole authority to nullify the unconstitutional or otherwise invalid actions of the other two branches. Nixon, with nicely balanced rhetoric, argued that the President could not tell the courts what to do, and therefore it was not "for the courts to seek to compel some particular action from the President." But that argument has been consistently rejected by every judge at every level.

Exercising this authority, the courts have placed certain limitations on presidential power, as indicated in Chapter 3; and the very existence of the courts is one important reason why the Presidency is not as omnipotent as commonly viewed. To be sure, chance and prosecutorial discretion determine which matters come before the courts for review; and a President about to lose a case can usually make it moot before it reaches the Supreme Court. Nevertheless when that Court does enter the picture, its entry, as in the Watergate matter, can be decisive.[1] Its unanimous decision in the Nixon tapes case, reflecting the views of the three Nixon appointees sitting as well as all others, could not be labeled by the President's most fervent defenders as an "eastern liberal establishment plot." Unlike the decisions of congressional committees and lower courts, its order enjoyed such great national respect that the President felt compelled to obey it—even to the point of turning over the particular tapes that sealed his fate.

The President in Court

The Nixon tapes case illustrates the role which the courts might have played in holding presidential power accountable over the years, had they always been this forthright and courageous in combatting presidential excesses. Unfortunately, when its record is examined in detail, the judiciary is seen to have contributed very little toward presidential accountability. Indeed its attitude toward the Presidency has, on the whole, been even more deferential than that of Congress. It approaches, wrote Emmet Hughes, "something of a study in institutional timidity."

Constitutional scholar Edwin Corwin wrote that "while the Court has sometimes rebuffed Presidential contentions, it has more often labored to rationalize them." Clinton Rossiter, in his invaluable *The American Presidency*, went even further:

For most practical purposes, the President may act as if the Supreme Court did not exist. . . . The fact is that the Court has done more over the years to expand than to contract the authority of the Presidency. . . . It is clearly one of the least reliable restraints on Presidential activity.

Even some of the Court's most famous rulings against

presidential power, earlier cited, fell short of imposing the meaningful curbs often attributed to them. A constitutional-law text setting forth the key rulings against the Presidency might well focus on the following seven cases:

(1) *Marbury* v. *Madison*,[2] in which John Marshall established the practice of judicial review of official acts. Yet Marshall actually ended up refusing, on jurisdictional grounds, to issue a writ of mandamus against the Executive.

(2) The subpoena of President Jefferson in *U.S.* v. *Burr*.[3] Yet full and final disclosure from Jefferson was not in the end required; and much of Marshall's *dicta* in that case has been interpreted to support an even wider executive privilege than the Court acknowledged in the *Nixon* case.

(3) *Ex Parte Milligan*,[4] long the favorite authority of those arguing for limited presidential powers, a Supreme Court decision in 1866 denying in sweeping language Abraham Lincoln's Civil War orders to suspend habeas corpus and institute martial law. But by 1866 the war was over and Lincoln was dead—and in all probability so was Milligan. (The government's brief acknowledged that as far as it knew he had been hanged the previous year by order of a military commission.) Three years earlier, when it would have mattered, the Court by a 5–4 vote in the *Prize Cases*[5] had declared that the outbreak of Civil War gave Lincoln—even prior to any congressional action—sweeping wartime authority as Commander-in-Chief not limited to his statutory powers against insurrection.

(4) The *Youngstown Steel Seizure* case,[6] in which the Supreme

Court by a 6–3 vote overturned President Truman's Korean War seizure of the nation's steel mills to prevent a strike. Yet the value of this decision as precedent is limited, partly because each of the six Justices in the majority wrote a separate opinion. No question was raised in any of them about President Truman's authority to declare an emergency or intervene in Korea in the first place without the consent of Congress. Indeed the majority would have been on the other side, a reading of the opinions makes clear, had Congress not specifically considered the seizure alternative when legislating in this area and rejected it in favor of other remedies.

(5) *The New York Times* v. *U.S..*,[7] a freedom of the press landmark in which the Court refused to enjoin publication of the Pentagon Papers notwithstanding the President's claim of national security. Here again the value of the decision as a restraint on future presidential action is weakened by the fact that every member of the Court felt compelled to issue an individual opinion.

(6) *U.S.* v. *U.S. District Court*,[8] in which the Court condemned wiretaps without court order in domestic "national security" cases. Unfortunately it explicitly avoided any judgment on wiretaps established for reasons of foreign intelligence, a gaping loophole in a country where everyone from Dean Acheson to Martin Luther King to Daniel Ellsberg has been accused by someone of links with an international communist network. Moreover, language in the opinion contained the unfortunate suggestion that the President's oath of office is enough to give him powers against subversive activities.

(7) Finally, *U.S.* v. *Nixon*.[9] It helped close down Watergate,

but it opened up—by its implicit endorsement of an unfettered presidential privilege of communication in the military and diplomatic area—a new can of worms for future courts and congressional committees. By stating flatly and unanimously that executive privilege is "intrinsically rooted" in our constitutional system, and suggesting that it may even be unreviewable by the courts if the President invokes national security, the Court cast a broad and simplistic gloss over long-debated questions that are certain to rise again in a context less obvious than that presented by the Nixon tapes case.

Thus these "landmarks" against excessive presidential power are dimmer than they should be. The real problem, however, is the score or more of key court rulings in favor of the President, each endorsing (as in the *Prize Cases* earlier mentioned) an expansion of his powers.

A study by Glendon Schubert of some 800 cases dealing with presidential power between 1790 and 1956 found only 38—or less than 5 percent—going against the President, and most of these on relatively minor points.[10] The Nixon tapes case was in fact the first time the Supreme Court had *directly* ordered any President to do anything.

Often the courts refuse to face an issue of presidential power on the legal merits, instead declaring it "political," moot, or inherently "executive" in nature, or finding that the plaintiffs have no standing, or that the courts have no jurisdiction, or that Congress had implicitly ratified the presidential action; or ruling that the suit is in reality one against the government without its consent (and thus barred), or that the intent of

Congress was unclear, or that the President's deviation from that intent is insignificant, or that the case could be decided on nonconstitutional grounds. There is usually a way to find in favor of the President, and the courts usually have.

• When the Navy under Franklin Pierce bombarded a Nicaraguan town into rubble because a crowd threw a bottle at an American diplomat, the courts ruled that the President's decision to take this congressionally unauthorized military action was conclusive.[11]

• When Grover Cleveland sought an injunction against Eugene Debs's strike against the Pullman Company, the Court said no statutory authority was required to do so.[12]

• When Theodore Roosevelt said he had the power to take the military action (and the land) he wanted for the Panama Canal,[13] and when Franklin Roosevelt said he had the power to reorganize government maritime agencies that had been established by Congress,[14] the courts acquiesced.

They also said that they had no power to enjoin a President in the performance of his official duties;[15] that the President has extensive powers to declare and combat emergencies, including the call-up of a state militia;[16] that his executive agreements with foreign governments[17] and his executive orders[18] have the force of law; that his power to pardon convicted or alleged criminals (presumably including ex-Presidents) is unlimited;[19] that the Constitution gives him sweeping powers beyond those spelled out explicitly;[20] that his war powers are virtually unreviewable,[21] and include the execution of alien saboteurs,[22] and that they can be extended into post-war periods;[23] that his action altering a regulatory agency decision certified to him for a final ruling is, unlike other quasi-judicial regulatory agency proceedings, unreviewable in court;[24] and that he can remove almost any executive department employee if he goes about it right.[25]

That is only the beginning. In language too broad, almost awestruck, to be taken altogether seriously, but which subsequent courts have nevertheless cited repeatedly, the Supreme Court in 1936 endowed the President with vast and virtually unlimited authority in foreign affairs in an opinion written by a former Senator, George Sutherland.[26]

The Court has consistently been more willing to restrain Congress or even itself than the President. It insisted in the early New Deal days that congressional delegations of power to the President were invalid if not sufficiently explicit or restricted.[27] But since the 1937 switch,[28] the courts have had no trouble finding all delegations valid. They have also consistently taken the President's side in upholding his interpretation of statutes to find powers not explicitly conferred upon him by Congress.[29]

By no means were all or even most of these cases wrong on the law or the merits. But all helped create the impression that the President was, in Justice Jackson's words, "relatively immune from judicial review." [30] They helped sanctify a dangerous mystique of infallible presidential power, particularly in alleged emergencies. And it was in that context that Franklin Roosevelt committed (with congressional as well as judicial approval) in the first year after Pearl Harbor one of this country's most shameful deeds—the relocation and confinement of more than 100,000 Americans of Japanese ancestry on ethnic grounds alone.[31]

The latest tragic result of the judiciary's reluctance to challenge the President was its posture on the Indochina war. At first the judicial branch refused even to consider the problem of the constitutionality of the President's decision to send troops into Vietnam, stating that it wanted to make clear to anyone "similarly inclined that resort to the courts is futile, in addition to being wasteful of time, for which there are urgent legitimate demands." [32] Then, in a long series of cases, a few lower federal courts slowly began to acknowledge that the President had no inherent power to wage war on his own, that at least some participation by the Congress in the decision was required, that the issue if properly framed was not necessarily political and was indeed justiciable—but that the Gulf of Tonkin Resolution, military appropriations, and related legislative enactments constituted sufficient congressional ratification.[33]

At last, in 1973, after repeal of the Tonkin Resolution, after the removal of American ground forces and prisoners, and after a clear expression of congressional disapproval of continued combat, the executive branch had run out of alleged legislative mandates. (One State Department spokesman, when asked in 1972 who or what authorized the bombing of Cambodia, could only reply: "The justification is the reelection of President Nixon.") An injunction against the further bombing of Cambodia was sought by New York Congresswoman Elizabeth Holtzman and several Air Force officers serving in Asia.[34] The same Federal District Court Judge before whom I had unsuccessfully argued the *Berk* case three years earlier decided this time to grant the injunction, concluding that the required congressional authorization for military activities in or over Cambodia did not exist.

But thereafter the pattern of judicial avoidance continued. The District Court's order was stayed by the Court of Appeals; Justice Douglas's vacating of that stay was overruled by a hastily polled full Supreme Court; and, only days before the bombing was to halt anyway by virtue of an Act of Congress, the Court of Appeals in a split decision said once again that this was a political, nonjusticiable issue.

These Indochina cases further blot a record already discouraging to anyone looking to the courts to hold the President accountable. (Nor is this record reassuring to those who hope that the requirement of a federal court order will prevent the unjustified use of "national security" wiretaps; or to those who hope that the new Freedom of Information Act amendments enabling federal judges to overrule "national security" secrecy claims will bring about the release of needlessly classified information.) To be sure, neither the language of the Constitution nor the historical and judicial precedents confronting the courts were wholly clear on the war power question. But however deliberately vague the framers may have left the line dividing the President's power to conduct war as Commander-in-Chief and the Congress's power to authorize war, they clearly did not intend to draw it completely on the side of the President—which is what the Cambodia bombing represented. Surely, as Justice Douglas noted in his review of the

Holtzman case, a court which in the *Steel Seizure* case could act boldly against a President to prevent him from unconstitutionally taking property in time of war should be able to prevent him from unconstitutionally taking lives.

It is precisely because periods of war and emergency are most likely to induce an extension or usurpation of presidential powers that those periods most require the objectivity, calm, and long-range view that the courts are particularly equipped to provide. Unfortunately those have been the very periods in our history when the courts have been most leery of asserting their authority over the President. "The Court's power of judicial review," wrote Rossiter in this context, "is least useful when most needed." Lamely but candidly the Court in *Ex Parte Milligan* rationalized its role:

During the late wicked Rebellion, the temper of the times did not allow that calmness in deliberation and discussion so necessary to a correct conclusion of a purely judicial question. . . . [F]eelings and interests prevailed which are happily terminated. *Now* that the public safety is assured, this question, as well as all others, can be discussed and decided without passion . . . .[35]

In similar fashion the Court in 1946 gingerly invalidated certain aspects of military rule in the Hawaiian Islands—after the war was over.[36] Thus is illustrated Justice Jackson's conclusion that the war power is the most dangerous of all to free government:

It usually is invoked in haste and excitement when calm legislative consideration of constitutional limitation is difficult. It is executed in a time of patriotic fervor that makes moderation unpopular. And, worst of all, it is interpreted by judges under the influence of the same passions and pressures.[37]

It is understandable that judges are reluctant to halt emergency or military actions without knowing all of the facts or consequences.

Judges, deficient in military knowledge, lacking vital information upon which to assess the nature of battlefield decisions, and sitting thousands of miles from the field of action, cannot reasonably or appropriately determine [the legality of] . . . a specific military operation . . . .[38]

But the Vietnam cases rarely called upon judges to pass on the wisdom of battlefield decisions as distinct from the existence of legal authority. The "allowable limits of military discretion," the Supreme Court was willing to state regarding a *Governor's* declaration of martial law during the depression, "and whether or not they have been overstepped in a particular case, *are judicial questions.*" [39] Moreover, Congress has recently rejected the Ford argument, in vetoing the Freedom of Information Act amendments, that judges "have no particular expertise" to review national security data.[40]

The doctrine that basic national policy and foreign policy decisions are reviewable only by the electorate and not by the courts, said Chief Judge Bazelon of the District of Columbia Court of Appeals in his dissent to an opinion rejecting Linus Pauling's challenge of nuclear testing, "attributes greater limitations to judicial power than the Constitution requires." [41]

Some have suggested that this record of reluctance to curb the President is an inevitable reaction on the part of judges who owe their appointments to the President. One may refute this cynical view by noting the number of judges who, aware of both their professional obligations and their lifetime tenure, have sorely disappointed the Presidents who appointed them. The District Court Judge who rejected Nixon's view in the *New York Times* case had been named by Nixon only a few weeks earlier. President Eisenhower is said to have regarded his selection of Chief Justice Earl Warren as his single biggest mistake. Although others regard it as his single biggest accomplishment, the point remains that Presidents do not enjoy their "relative immunity from judicial review" because of the personal gratitude or devotion of their appointees.

A more likely motivation is institutional self-interest, a desire on the part of the courts to avoid a showdown with the President for fear that he will ignore their orders and thereby weaken the unique standing of the judiciary. (In other words, "he's got the Army, Navy, and Air Force, and all we have is the Clerk of the Court.") But no President has yet *directly* defied an order of the *Supreme Court*—not feisty Harry Truman, not Franklin Roosevelt at the peak of his power, and not even Richard Nixon who knew that compliance could suddenly dispatch him to San Clemente. Indeed, the Court in the *Nixon* case ignored a clear hint that he might not comply.

There is no denying the fact that Lincoln defied the lower federal courts in the early days of the Civil War; and this may have induced the Supreme Court to act, while the war raged and Lincoln lived, with the pusillanimity earlier noted. In 1861, when the District of Columbia Circuit Court was engaged in a dispute with the local Provost Marshal, General

Porter, over the right of habeas corpus of military prisoners, Lincoln personally ordered the Court's Deputy Marshal not to serve its show-cause order on Porter. The Court yielded, but with stinging language:

. . . the case presented is without a parallel in the judicial history of the United States, and involves the free action and efficiency of the judges of this court. The president, charged by the constitution to take care that the laws be executed, has seen fit to arrest the process of this court . . . we have no physical power to enforce the lawful process of this court on his military subordinates against the president's prohibition.[42]

In that same year, Chief Justice Taney, sitting as a Circuit Judge, held in *Ex Parte Merryman*[43] that the war did not give Lincoln the power to suspend the writ of habeas corpus. In the face of military disregard of his decision, he added:

I have exercised all the power which the Constitution and laws confer upon me, but that power has been resisted by a force too strong for me to overcome;

and he ordered that a copy of the proceedings and his opinion be transmitted to the President in the hopes that he would fulfill "his constitutional obligation 'to take care that the laws be faithfully executed' . . . ." Lincoln, without freeing Merryman, did subsequently ask Congress for the necessary legislation, acknowledging that the legality of his actions had been challenged.

While the courts did not have their way against Lincoln, they lost no honor or stature in these confrontations. Surely the judicial branch will lose more standing and respect if it too often ducks important tests of presidential authority. "To deny inquiry into the President's power in a case like this, because of the damage to the public interest to be feared from upsetting its exercise by him," as Justice Frankfurter said concurring in the *Steel Seizure* case, "would in effect always preclude inquiry into challenged power . . . ." [44]

The courts have successfully ordered Congress to seat an ousted member.[45] They have not hesitated to issue orders to defiant Governors,[46] federal administrators, and military commanders.[47] But too often they have treated the occupant of the Oval Office with more than the "high degree of respect due the President of the United States." [48] They have exhibited instead the same degree of undue deference that Congress and the public have exhibited in aggrandizing presidential power and mystique.

If the President states that he has made a requisite finding, the courts have repeatedly held that he must be conclusively presumed to have done so, whether or not the time or evidence available to him appear supportive of such a finding.[49] On questions of power, declared Justice Story in 1827, the Court cannot apply to

the chief magistrate of the Union . . . the same principles . . . as might be applied to the humblest officer in the government. . . . When the President exercises an authority confided to him by law, the presumption is that it is exercised in pursuance of law.[50]

The courts cannot proceed against the President, said John Marshall in the *Burr* case, "as against an ordinary individual," and therefore "much reliance must be placed on the declaration of the President" as to his motives for not disclosing certain items.[51]

These are noble but unnecessary sentiments. They illustrate that:

The opinions of judges, no less than executives and publicists, often suffer the infirmity . . . of confounding the permanent executive office with its temporary occupant.[52]

Surely history has taught us that Presidents can be corrupt or overly ambitious, and that we do better to rely on the basic rule of American jurisprudence that no man, great or small, is above the law or entitled to preferential treatment.

If the courts, in this post-Watergate era of reappraisal, are to play their necessary and proper role in holding presidential power accountable between elections and without impeachment, they must examine the validity of their own motives when tempted to equivocate on questions of presidential power. Are they acting prudently and with restraint to avoid "government by lawsuit" and judicial supervision of a President who represents the will of the people? Or have they, too, been unduly awed by some President's invocation of the magical words "national security"? Is the particular issue before them purely political, for the electorate or Congress to decide? Or are there "judicially manageable standards" [53] on that issue which would enable them to hold the President legally accountable to his constitutional obligations?

It is to be hoped that members of the judicial branch, encouraged by the recent welter of holdings against the President, including the unanimous decision in *Nixon*, might now well resolve to shrink less often from confrontations with the Chief Magistrate, to treat him no differently than the "humblest officer in the government" or any other "ordinary individual," and not to be fearful of constitutional challenges to his foreign policy or emergency powers. They should feel free to rule against the Executive on sensitive or complex questions of degree or interpretation with the same confidence that they already rule against the legislative branch on such questions. Without attempting to command or enjoin acts of presidential discretion that "are only politically examinable," [54] they should, in short, exercise all of the judicial power conferred by the Constitution in order to keep their place in the federal balance of power.

Congress in Court

It should not be necessary, nor is it desirable for Congress to rely heavily or frequently on the courts to assert its own place in the balance of power. It was not the intention of the framers that the legislative branch or individual legislators be required to secure their rights against the executive branch by invoking the role of the judicial branch. Comity is a more flexible and constructive approach to executive-legislative relations than litigation can ever be. For example, a determination of which executive branch officials can invoke executive privilege, and on what kinds of matters and within what limitations, can better be worked out between Congress and the President than fought out in court.

Nevertheless suits against the executive branch by Congress and its individual members are no longer rarities, and as a last resort may be a necessity. The courts in recent decisions, although again with some hesitation, have recognized the standing of such plaintiffs. Congressmen are not only citizens and taxpayers, with such standing to sue as that may give them—they also have special rights concomitant with their special responsibilities to vote on impeachment, appropriations, and other matters dependent on the lawfulness of executive action or on their access to executive information.[55]

Yet special legislation was required to enable the Senate Watergate Committee to sue in its own name for certain presidential tapes that had been withheld. In the many suits brought by individual Senators and Representatives testing the legality of presidential actions, the legislator involved either acted as his own lawyer (thereby risking invocation of a familiar legal maxim) or depended upon private lawyers for whom private funds had to be raised.

With this background, the final report of the Ervin Committee sensibly recommended that Congress establish its own permanent legal service to assert its interests in court. It also urged legislation specifically giving the U.S. District Court in Washington, D.C., jurisdiction over suits brought by Congress in its own name to enforce its subpoenas against recalcitrant members of the executive branch, including the President.

Such legislation is desirable, not to encourage lawsuits by legislators, but to make certain this option is available when required. Only in this way can the limits of executive privilege, executive agreements, or some other executive power be defined if comity on these matters should break down under circumstances in which the weapons of Congress previously cited—such as the power to withhold confirmations, condition appropriations, and subpoena information—are not adequate or appropriate. Only in this way can the judicial process be fully utilized, if necessary, to secure the role of Congress and help give it the tools required to hold the President accountable.

The Department of Justice in Court

Even more important to judicial enforcement of presidential accountability were the Senate Watergate Committee's recommendations regarding a Special Prosecutor and the Department of Justice. There is wide support behind the proposal for a permanent office of Special Prosecutor, an independent "public attorney" or "Counsel General." With a fixed term longer than the President's, and subject to Senate confirmation, this individual's sole duties would be to investigate and prosecute official crimes—corruption, bribery, conflicts of interest, electoral abuses, and other wrongdoing, preferably in all three branches of the federal government—and to audit the administration of justice in other agencies.

The support for this proposal is understandable. To leave the prosecution of White House crimes, or other crimes by federal appointees, to an Attorney General selected by that White House, no matter how conscientious and nonpartisan he may be, does not build confidence in our system of justice. The mere existence of such a special office may help deter illegal activities on the part of an official who might otherwise assume that his possession of a White House telephone or tie clasp is sufficient assurance that his deeds will go undetected or unpunished. Those who say that such a prosecutor would have nothing to do in between semicentennial scandals forget that crimes high and low have been charged against officials in one or the other of the three branches of government in virtually every period of our history. Nor, given the remarkable effectiveness of Messrs. Cox and Jaworski and their tenacious aides, can we count on the next President under suspicion being willing to appoint a Special Prosecutor.

But upon further reflection I am concerned about the real dangers in this proposal. Until the ground rules for naming, confirming, supervising, staffing, financing, and removing such a prosecutor, along with the charter of his authority, have been carefully thought through to reduce these dangers—and thus far they have not been—action on this matter should be postponed. The power to accuse a President or to indict a federal official —even if a judge or jury throws the case out as baseless—is an enormous and sensitive power. Having observed how difficult it was, as a matter of political reality, to dislodge J. Edgar Hoover as FBI Director once he had built his reputation (and his files), and having observed how easy it was for a Joe McCarthy or Jim Garrison to make reckless accusations in order to stay in the limelight, this country does not now want an inquisitor so insulated from politics that his own unaccountability is more dangerous than the President's.

Watergate has also given rise to a number of proposals to insulate the Attorney General himself and the Department of Justice from politics. This too is understandable. The public cannot fully respect a government in which the President's chief legal adviser serves simultaneously as his chief political adviser and patronage dispenser. Nor can court decisions limiting presidential power have their intended effect on future Presidents if the legal advice received by those Presidents dilutes the meaning or applicability of those decisions for political reasons.

White House attempts to meddle on partisan grounds in the Justice Department's law enforcement functions must be prevented. Even if official crimes were left to a Special Prosecutor, the Attorney General's decisions on the prosecution of any kind of case should never be based on considerations of party affiliation, campaign contributions, or anything other than the merits.

In pursuit of this objective, all Department of Justice personnel from top to bottom should be prohibited from engaging in political activity, exempted from political clearance appointment procedures, and required to make maximum disclosure of all the requests and contacts they receive regarding pending matters from noninvolved third parties, including the White House and Congress. All U.S. Attorneys and Marshals should be removed from the political patronage system and appointed from a career service for longer terms by the Attorney General. Either a statute or the Senate confirmation process should bar anyone from serving as Attorney General who does not pledge to discontinue his political activities during his service in the Cabinet and for a prudent period thereafter.

But many of the post-Watergate proposals for an independent, nonpolitical Department of Justice, which would go far beyond the above steps, are wholly unrealistic. To call, as Senator Lowell Weicker has, for a separately elected Attorney General (who presumably would raise his own campaign funds!) is to ignore the many administrative functions of the Department and to guarantee an increase in its politicization. A Francis Biddle would never be elected Attorney General; a George Wallace might.

The Weicker proposal, like the Ervin proposal for an independent Attorney General whose fixed term goes beyond the President's, would fragment responsibility for law enforcement, and enable the Justice Department to ignore the views of the President and other executive departments on issues that are properly "political" issues (in the sense that presidential policy-making reflecting the interests and consent of the governed is appropriate)—civil rights, antitrust, anti-pollution enforcement, prison reform, narcotics, consumerism, and a host of others.

While Nixon went to one extreme in staffing the upper echelons of the Department almost entirely with politicians, former Attorney General Ramsey Clark went to the other in recently proposing to bar anyone from a top Justice Department post if he had previously run for elective office. That would let in John Mitchell and Robert Mardian and keep out Elliot Richardson, William Ruckelshaus, and (hereafter) Ramsey Clark. Politicians, as previously noted, can often stand up to a President and resist improprieties with more confidence than anonymities can. Some active politicians and presidential campaign aides have proven to be distinguished, nonpartisan Attorney Generals in the past. Some have not. It is professional character and wisdom that count, and no automatic bar on politicians can provide that.

Nevertheless, Weicker, Ervin, Clark, and others are right in rejecting the oft-voiced assumption that the events of the past two years are enough to halt similar evils in our system of justice for some time. "Watergate," said the Senate Watergate Committee Report, "at least teaches that the abuse of power must be anticipated." Changes in the posture of our courts and law enforcement machinery must be undertaken to detect, correct, and to the extent possible prevent those abuses in the future. But as was said by Robert Jackson, whose service in both the Department of Justice and on the High Court gave him special insight into these matters:

The chief restraint upon those who command the physical forces of the country, in the future as in the past, must be their responsibility to the political judgments of their contemporaries and to the moral judgments of history.[56]

With that observation in mind, we turn in our final chapter to an examination of how best to enhance those political and moral judgments.

8
Making the President
More Accountable to the People

. . . at least 50% of the American people will always believe
what any President tells them because they want to believe
what any President tells them. If the President goes on TV
and makes a flat-out statement, people tend to want to believe
it. They will still answer questions in polls that the government
is not telling them all . . . but they nonetheless will believe the
President.

> Memorandum from Nixon Counsel Charles Colson
> to Chief of Staff H. R. Haldeman

The Colson observation is not only a useful insight into the
Watergate cover-up, but also is unfortunately true. The undue
deference to the Presidency which has weakened the roles of
Congress and the courts in holding that office accountable is
only a mild reflection of the undue reverence which most
Americans have traditionally paid to both the office and each
new occupant. Even as cynicism about presidential politics
and dispiritedness about the American system increase, a large
proportion of the population under normal conditions wants
desperately to believe whatever the President tells them,
particularly at the start of his term, and to support all requests
by that President made in the name of national security.

The Mystique of the President

Before election he is a politician, a particularly scorned species
in American life, subject to the harshest challenge and

examination. After inauguration, wrapped in the flag and stamped with the great seal, he heads America's only royal family, his actions at least initially immune from reprobation, his decisions endowed with magical wisdom. Gerald Ford's presidential honeymoon ended almost before the rice was out of his top hat. But for one month a grateful public, as reflected in the mass media, awakening from its long national nightmare, adored his every word. "[N]ot mystique but candor, not majesty but humility, not complexity but plainness," wrote one normally skeptical columnist.

A national survey in 1962 ascertained that most American school children regarded the President as "omniscient, omnipotent, and infallible." [1] Clearly so did many adults. The President at that time was a great man, but he had none of those qualities. I saw no halo, I observed no mystery. And yet I found that my own personal, highly informal relationship with him changed as soon as he entered the Oval Office.

He was the same human being with the same faults and virtues with whom I had worked, joked, argued, and traveled, almost night and day, for eight years. Yet my attitude was instantly characterized by a greater degree of not only deference but awe. Addressing him at all times, at play as well as work, as "Mr. President" instead of the former "Jack" was but a symbol of this change. I noted a similar alteration in the attitudes of his other staff members, his old friends, his seniors in the Congress, and even his political enemies.

Thomas Jefferson knew that President Jefferson was but a temporary servant of the people, and after his inauguration he stood to wait for a place at his boarding house table. A modern President, if he is wise, will know from the experiences of Nixon, Johnson, Truman, and others that the obeisance initially received from a large segment of the public is only a temporary phenomenon—that he must earn genuine respect through his actions lest a still larger segment of the public turn on him.

Yet not even the humblest new President (of course, no truly humble man has been elected President in this century) could resist a feeling that perhaps all this adulation was deserved, and that his judgment was in fact infallible. With Congress enjoying no such personal acclaim, with his critics looking like shrill or unpatriotic malcontents, a new President's accountability is thus dangerously low. Not surprisingly, Kennedy blundered during such a period into the Bay of Pigs, Ford stumbled over the Nixon pardon, and Truman too abruptly ended lend-lease. The resulting shock of reality was healthy for them and for the country. A Presidency that is viewed by both the public and its occupant as larger than life can soon tempt that occupant to feel larger than the law.

Even Presidents no longer new or widely revered have continued to occupy a position so high in our national system of values and emotions that a substantial portion of the American people never could bring themselves to reject them. The American Revolution produced an office that may be treated with less adoration than that of king but it is certainly treated with more veneration than that of prime minister. Knowledge of Eisenhower's intestinal tract and Johnson's abdominal scar did not alter this pattern of homage. Mass media coverage of the Presidency brought familiarity, but not contempt.

In part, this public attitude reflects a craving for superheroes and father figures as strong among many Americans as it is among the citizens of any monarchy. In part, as Michael Novak has written, it is a compulsion to trust the President as the principal symbol by which we identify ourselves and our country. In part it is because all recent Presidents—not merely Nixon—have sought to invest their persons with the hallowed traditions and trappings of their office, drawing upon the glamour of their official residences, limousines, yachts, and ceremonies.

Finally, this attitude is due in part to one of our most treasured and reassuring myths about the Presidency—the myth that the office ennobles the man, and that a little man will grow in the White House to be a giant if the times require it. Nixon, Grant, and Harding did not grow, they shrank. An individual subject to the demands of that unique office is likely to have his weaknesses magnified instead of his strengths, to fall victim to megalomania or paranoia or both. Contrary to populist sentiment, an ordinary man cannot handle the job. The Civil War may have revealed the real strength of Lincoln, but the Great Depression revealed the real strength of Hoover.

I hope that the events of the past year have enabled most Americans to distinguish the occupant from the office, remaining respectful of the latter while skeptical of the former. Even the office could do with less pomp. "Hail to the Chief" is not all that melodic, and fewer jets, yachts, and uniformed aides would be more consistent with Jefferson's boarding-house image.

The plain and open style of President Ford may be a sign that these changes are taking hold. Certainly the published transcripts of Oval Office conversations between Mr. Nixon and his staff (conducted largely in subbasic English, cynical press agentry jargon, and undeleted expletives) should have opened many eyes—not only to the crimes under discussion, but also to the lack of anything inherently grand or noble in presidential deliberations. The next time anyone refers to the glory and majesty of the Presidency as though every occupant of the office has mounted a pedestal, let him remember the Nixon tapes.

One of the worst by-products of the presidential mystique is the myth that only the President possesses the information to decide what the national security requires. That myth helped get this country into Vietnam and helped get Nixon's aides into jail. "The very words [national security] served to block critical analysis," said Egil Krough, in explaining his willingness to help plan the burglary of Ellsberg's psychiatrist. In truth the secret reports to at least three Presidents on Vietnam—from military and diplomatic officials telling those Presidents what those officials wanted them to hear—were not as sound a basis for national security judgments as many of the press reports and scholarly studies available to the general population.

If as a result of Watergate and Vietnam more Americans will look more skeptically at every President—forgetting about the mystique and the majesty, requiring him to earn and deserve their respect, and making him prove that the national security is at stake when he invokes it—they will surely be better able to hold him accountable.

The Media and the President

The electorate's principal agent in examining presidential power and character must be the news media. Few reporters today regard any President or presidential prospect with undue deference or blindly accept his word on national security or any other subject. But some of them (and their editors) are more interested in the sensational than the complex, in examining a candidate's private life instead of his private thoughts, or in reporting fully on his bankbook and teeth instead of his operating philosophy and political habits. They build up a "cult of personality" for a popular President, and the "credibility gap" of an unpopular one, largely ignoring the important but more subtle role of institutions and processes.

Some, lacking the necessary time or interest, merely imitate what their colleagues are saying on a new presidential proposal or reword a government agency handout on the subject, instead of immersing themselves in the facts in order to give their readers or viewers an in-depth perspective. Some of their publishers are more responsive to the wishes of advertisers than to the need for more Washington and foreign-affairs coverage. Too many Americans now live in one-newspaper towns, where the lack of competition diminishes both the opportunity to correct errors and the attention paid to a reporter's professional qualifications. Yet other Americans who try to follow public affairs closely are subject to such a barrage of instant, undigested, miscellaneous information and sensations filtered through the selection process of news editors, producers, or reporters that they simply lack the time and means to sort it all out.

Yet the news media's impact is all-powerful, particularly in the case of television. Its enormous influence on the public mind makes Presidents not only fearful of its scrutiny but also covetous of its power. Not even the most partisan daily newspaper today would turn its pages over to the President to fill as he wished without giving some opportunity to the opposition to be heard. Yet it is not uncommon for the President even in an election year to preempt on his own say-so prime time on all three television networks to present his side of a current debate without any assurance that a spokesman for the other side will be heard.

The networks should and will cover all newsworthy events, including major presidential declarations; and the "equal time" rule, the FCC's "Fairness Doctrine," and each network's news judgment are usually sufficient to assure televised replies from the opposition when appropriate in those situations. But a policy of resistance to the mystique of the Presidency should also enable any network, backed by a truly independent FCC and statute if necessary, to decline to carry live and in full any presidential address that it has not ascertained in advance to be newsworthy; and to insist, if the President still insists, that only one of the three networks carry that address (this to be done on a rotating basis), with the assurance of equal time from the opposition point of view. Even with a statute, this will require more backbone in the network back rooms. Inasmuch as spokesmen for Congress and the opposition party are unlikely ever to command the attention given the President, the networks must be sparing in their willingness to grant him this advantage.

In short, despite the valuable role already played by the news media in enabling the American people to hold the President accountable, that role should be strengthened still further. Some honest and able individuals, unwilling for family or other reasons to subject their lives to the pitiless scrutiny of the post-Watergate press, may thus be deterred from seeking high office, including the Presidency. Some who do will undoubtedly endure needless pain from stories unrelated to their fitness for office. But these disadvantages pale in comparison with the dangers of a servile or listless press. The news media, contrary to the oft-repeated assertion, did not bring Nixon down. They merely revealed and reported what he and his aides had said and done that merited their downfall; and we would be a more vulnerable nation by far if a public weary of controversy accepted any limitation on journalism's probing eye, whatever its motes and beams.

The Marketing of the President

Contrary to the pessimistic view often expressed (by young citizens in particular), the people can help hold a President accountable by making their voice heard between presidential elections—in congressional and local elections, in letters, telegrams, and telephone calls to the White House, in public opinion polls, in messages to the media, in influencing the statements of opinion leaders, in organizing protests, changing parties, or swelling the ranks of some movement. Both Lyndon Johnson and Richard Nixon felt the power of public opinion between elections. As George Wallace would say: "Send him a message." To which I would add: feel free to call him by his first name.

But clearly the American public's most direct and important opportunity to supervise a President's power should be the election process that makes him President. Unfortunately the typically frenetic but skillfully packaged and merchandised presidential campaign is unlikely to enable voters to obtain either maximum leverage on the White House or even reliable knowledge of each candidate's perception of presidential power and purpose. Television may have increased the amount of campaign information easily available about the candidate. But it has also increased the number of campaign distortions. If current Federal Trade Commission rules against unsubstantiated claims and false or misleading representations were applicable, they would eliminate or tone down substantial portions of most political advertisements, to say nothing of political speeches (including some I have written).

I hope that the advent of public financing for presidential elections—which Nixon opposed as "undermining the very foundation of our democratic process"—will, while not graft-proof, substantially lessen the most glaring distortions in our election system: those caused by money. For at least the last 30 years of presidential politics, money has equalled power. The total spent far exceeded the amount required for the legitimate education of the electorate. It bought for the candidate computerized direct mail assaults and television commercials that attempted to create "charisma" and occasionally summarize the issues in one page—or 60 seconds—of cliches, slogans, and stereotypes. It bought for the large contributor extra access to the candidate, extra influence in the outcome of the election, and sometimes something more.

This combination of political power with economic power was unhealthy for all but the donor. The illegal contributions to the Nixon campaign by the milk producers were small compared to the direct economic benefits they received from the American public as a result of higher dairy support prices and lower import quotas. But even at the other end of the scale, not one of the many scrupulously honest and ethical elected officials I have known could avoid an unconscious tendency to treat differently, to greet a little more warmly, or to hear out a little more solicitously a visitor to his office who had made a major campaign contribution in comparison with a constituent who had not.

The new public financing law, accompanied by new restrictions on campaign contributions and spending, should, if vigorously enforced, change all that (and as a by-product substantially improve the quality of American Ambassadors abroad). In addition, Congress should amend the Federal Communications Act to provide ample free television time to presidential nominees, conditioning it upon their participation in a series of televised debates. The Kennedy-Nixon debates of 1960, though sometimes highlighting such less-than-momentous issues as Quemoy and Matsu and Harry T. profanity, were with all their faults an extraordinarily s ful means of informing and involving the electorate—v may be why there has never been another such debate.

Presidential elections will remain inadequate instruments accountability, however, until citizens of every age, race, anc economic bracket are able to perceive a closer connection between their participation in that process and the performance of the President. That requires stronger, not weaker, political parties—meaningful grass-roots party organizations, open equally to everyone, serving as nationwide two-way communications vehicles which link the President or presidential candidate and his platform with all state and local party members, officials, and candidates and their platforms. It also requires an increased, not diminished, role for broad-based party leaders in the selection of presidential candidates and the conduct of their campaigns.

Unfortunately, the country has been moving in the opposite direction. Presidential nominees have bypassed party machinery to establish personal campaign organizations such as Nixon's CREEP. Incumbent Presidents have all but ignored their National Committee Chairmen, yet submerged their own responsibilities as party leaders. Many of the new campaign reforms emphasize still more "popularity contest" primaries instead of better conventions, personal campaign finance committees instead of party treasurers, and transient volunteers instead of organization regulars.

Party identification and loyalty in our increasingly affluent, educated, and mass-media-oriented country have already to their lowest level. Recent foolish talk about a nent third (or fourth) party movement can only weaken urther the effectiveness of the existing parties as instruments of political expression and accountability. Although ird and fourth parties born of past national conflicts have occasionally succeeded in a single election year in dramatizing neglected issues and compelling the major parties to adopt some of their ideas, their continued presence on the scene is likely to create more opportunities for mischievous disruption and minority-rule manipulation (as in New York State) than for intellectual stimulation. Recurrent proposals for a national presidential primary offer a similar threat. By virtually eliminating any exercise of discretion by party leaders and delegates—who can take a view beyond the popularity contest—a national primary would wholly cripple party viability.

To be sure, politics and parties, because of Watergate, are now deemed dirtier than ever by many people. But it was not the Republican National Committee that broke the locks and the law at Watergate. (Former Republican Chairman Robert Dole has observed that his party was not only not involved in Watergate in 1972, it was not involved in the convention, campaign, election, or inauguration.) Professional political leaders and institutions who year after year must appeal to the public and work with the opposition are less likely than temporary collections of amateurs to subvert competing professionals and institutions.

The two-party system and the parties themselves should be important instruments of presidential accountability. They can be only if representative party leaders can reverse these present trends and start playing the role originally intended for presidential electors—the role of developing, screening, nominating, electing, counseling, and if necessary checking a President who is representative of their membership.

The Measuring of the President

But can party leaders or voters, before they are committed to a particular candidate for the Presidency, determine the likelihood of his abusing his powers? As only one of many criteria in judging a prospective President, that question is likely to be overlooked in the attention paid to such other factors (all related to his use or abuse of power) as his politics, competence, character, experience, personality, and position on the issues.

There is always a temptation, especially on the part of party leaders, to assume that the candidate who can win can also govern. In truth the qualities required for these two tasks have over the last generation had less and less in common. There is also a temptation to apply one set of standards to one's own candidate, and another set to his opponents. But it was precisely that kind of double standard among thoughtful Republicans and conservatives that kept Nixon on the national stage for too many years.

The psychiatric screening of presidential candidates by either medical men or politicians is unrealistic. Doctors are not trained to distinguish between a candidate's positions on executive power and executive privilege, and politicians are not trained to tell the difference between paranoia and phlebitis. "The line dividing good and evil does not run between states, classes or parties," Alexander Solzhenitsyn has written, "it runs through every human heart." There is good and evil in the heart of every presidential candidate; and what is needed is some basis for predicting which will predominate in the White House.

Let the buyer beware. All candidates, particularly after Watergate, will solemnly pledge restraint, openness, humility, and cooperation with Congress. They always have. "I don't want a government of yes-men" is a sample pledge from the same candidate who later felt compelled as President to give us his equally credible assurance: "I am not a crook."

Nevertheless there are at least four specific clues to the future that can be examined before voters finally commit themselves. First, a candidate's political operating style will tell us something of his capacity to respond to the democratic process as well as use it. One whose campaign consistently conceals, denies, or distorts facts, or presents a different face to different audiences, is more likely to lie as President than one whose exaggerations and fakery are at least within the traditional American norms of what Wendell Willkie dismissed as "campaign oratory."

A candidate who has a sense of humor and a sense of history, a willingness to listen and to learn and to debate his opponent, an ability to accommodate and to negotiate, and a capacity to get some joy out of politics and some joy out of life, is unlikely to bring on a new Watergate. But one who seeks the nomination by high-handed, win-at-any-price tactics, relying more on his political technique than on his substantive judgment, and more on appeals to prejudice and pocketbooks than on the force of his arguments, should not be readily entrusted with the power to do this country great harm.

A candidate's reaction to criticism and particularly to adversity—such as losing a state primary or losing his first try for the Presidency—will tell more than his reaction to success. The rigid, single-minded candidate who blames everyone else for his setbacks and makes no changes in his own approach could well turn out to be an equally arbitrary and isolated President. Even the most responsible presidential campaign is an arduous ordeal that discourages all but the most hardy practicing politicians from undertaking it, thus narrowing our choice. But it is nevertheless an important testing-ground for both the candidates and the country.

A second clue is the prospect's relationship with the news media. If his press conferences are frequent, frank, informal, and informative events, containing an occasional "I don't know" or "I was wrong," that candidate is more likely as President to be accessible not only to the press but also to the Cabinet, Congress, party leaders, and public. Accessibility and accountability are intertwined. Seclusive isolation impaired the sense of reality of both of Mr. Ford's predecessors. A wise President must be accessible to, and want access to, all different kinds of ideas, contacts, and reading matter, including the unofficial and unscreened.

Third, one can gain some notion of a future President's Cabinet by his selection of the first member of that Cabinet — his Vice President. A good case can be made for abolishing

that inevitably unhappy and unsatisfying office and placing
the Speaker of the House, President *Pro Tem* of the Senate or
Secretary of State next in line, to serve out a departed
President's term or until a new one can be elected.[2] But the
country seems wedded to the notion of having, in the event of
presidential death, disability, conviction after impeachment,
or resignation, an immediate successor clothed in the legiti-
macy of a regular national election.

A presidential nominee who selects a weak, little-known
running mate with no proven ability or national constituency
is unlikely to select a strong Cabinet. But a presidential
nominee who selects for the second spot a nationally known
figure with whom he can work, and whom he permits to take
some initiatives during the campaign, is more likely to appoint
department heads of outstanding ability who will enjoy some
leeway in administering their areas of responsibility.

Every post-war President except Eisenhower either served
first as Vice President or (in Kennedy's case) first came to
national prominence as a vice-presidential prospect. The traits
of all vice-presidential possibilities should therefore be examined as closely as those of the presidential contenders. The
Agnew and Eagleton episodes were unnecessary reminders
that the vice-presidential selection should no longer be hastily
and tardily made for ticket-balancing reasons by an exhausted
presidential nominee in the virtually mindless closing hours of
his party's convention.

Not all of the changes suggested for picking a Vice President
would be improvements. A presidential candidate should not
be required to select and run with his vice-presidential choice

from the earliest primaries onward, even before he knows who among the presidential contenders will be available or what kind of running-mate will be needed to unite the party after his nomination. Nor should each vice-presidential candidate be required to campaign on his own in the primaries and be nominated or elected separately, regardless of the presidential nominee's ability to trust and work with him.

But some alternative which facilitates more deliberate choice, complete with screening by both the presidential nominee and his party after the convention trauma is over, should be developed. A Vice President chosen with greater care and enjoying greater presidential confidence can strengthen the President's Cabinet, his links with Congress and the country, and his range of advice without interfering in the slightest with the Vice President's only two constitutional duties: presiding over the Senate when he feels like it, and inquiring each morning after the President's health. It should not require a constitutional amendment to make possible a more constructive use of his talents.

A fourth and final clue about a future President's behavior in office is provided by his campaign staff. Most of a candidate's key aides and advisers on the long road to nomination and election will, if he is successful, move into the White House and administration with him. That is not a harmful tradition. To avoid isolation from political reality, a President needs a staff with political and governmental experience—particularly Washington experience. In the Nixon White House, according to Herb Klein, "Most of the President's advisers who had real political experience and

talent found that they were allowed little or no access to him."
What type took their place? "I had a lot to learn about
government," recently acknowledged one of Haldeman's top-
most and toughest aides, Fred Malek.

I didn't know a liberal from a conservative. I didn't understand that Congress made the laws and the Executive executed
them.

In Washington, access is power. It is the stock-in-trade of
the most sought-after lobbyists and successful columnists.
Those who can gain the ear of power appear to possess it
themselves. This is even more true in the White House. Those
aides who are known to see the President regularly and
informally are presumed to be influencing him and to have the
right to speak for him—partly because those who do not,
including other staff members and department heads, are
afraid to test the validity of those presumptions.

A certain jockeying for direct and frequent access to the
Oval Office is thus inevitable in every White House. Some
assistants and advisers work on their relationship with the
President, or his personal secretary or his appointments aide;
others depend on their knowledge of his schedule or his
interests. (When the President occasionally comes to *your*
office, that's power.) When access is controlled by a hard-
nosed Chief of Staff like Haldeman, who gradually drove out
of the White House inner circle those with a philosophy or
background different from his own, the President is less likely
to hear the fresh and varied viewpoints, including bad news
and constructive criticisms, that he desperately needs to hear.

"Now you will never hear the truth again," Henry Manning said he was told upon his election as Cardinal-Archbishop of Westminster, adding on his own:

Everybody in high place stands in a room full of mirrors and sees himself multiplied without end by a servile reflection.

To obtain a closer view of a presidential candidate, the voters, with the aid of the press, should examine his reflection in his staff.

Examine also his relations with them. Do they advise as well as consent, tell him when he is wrong as well as right? LBJ's talented White House aides were more open and accessible than he was. But when, upon my submission of a letter of resignation, he assured me "I treat my staff like they were my own children," I knew I was right in moving out.

Watching with horror and sorrow as the Nixon staff sank in a paroxysm of accusations, confessions, indictments, and resignations, I could not help but meditate on whether the Kennedy staff could have ended up similarly and why they did not. It was not because Kennedy chose to hire more academicians and lawyers than Nixon did; even "the best and the brightest" have their limitations, as the sorry history of Vietnam illustrates. Nor was it because Kennedy appointees were on the whole younger than Nixon's—we were not. We had in fact several characteristics in common with the considerably larger yet less diverse Nixon staff. We, too, were intensely loyal, committed to our chief and determined upon his success. We, too, were guilty at least occasionally of what Hamlet called "the insolence of office," the curt or uncompromising demand or answer, the unwillingness to give that extra minute or word that reduces friction between the wheels of government.

But the staff, I note again, is a reflection of the President. Nixon's aides, according to the testimony of one of them, Hugh Sloan,

believed they were entitled to do things differently, to suspend the rules, because they were fulfilling a mission.

We believed we were obligated to do things carefully, to follow the rules, because we were fulfilling a mission. Different Presidents project different missions.

I offer these comparisons not to boast of the past or to ignore its shortcomings, but to offer some guideposts for the future. If the principal members of a presidential candidate's campaign staff—as reported by the press or as observed by party leaders—are a homogeneous group of sycophants obsessed with secrecy and with the pleasures rather than the purposes of power, if their skills lie more in staging motorcades or telethons than in amending legislation or communicating public policy, then that tells us little about them but speaks volumes about him. That is not guilt by association. A President must be judged in part on whom he is willing to take into his house, there to invoke his name and use his telephone—and affect our lives.

In the final analysis, the kind of President we get depends on the kind of government we want. If we want a government that safeguards human rights, suppresses venal conduct, and intervenes in an open and humanitarian way in the life of our country, then we should be able to find and elect a President capable of exercising strong, progressive leadership that is fully accountable. Many people do not want that kind of leadership or government. Preferring a more conservative, *laissez-faire* approach, they now seize upon Watergate to urge a less powerful and more passive Presidency.

To be sure, the American citizenry must not continue to impose excessive demands upon its Presidents, to hold them responsible for the fall of every sparrow, to expect of them constant new triumphs and bold Grand Designs. But it would be tragic for this country if Congress, the courts, and the American public used the powers set forth above to hold the President accountable in a way that rendered him impotent. Our objective instead should be to preserve the essence of presidential power while preventing its excesses, to entrust to the office the capacity to do great good without our having to fear great harm.

Some may be disappointed that this book does not suggest more statutory solutions. But I have tried to stress that we cannot rely on new laws alone to keep presidential leadership within ethical and constitutional bounds. Realistically speaking, ours is a government of men as well as laws; and men can always find ways to avoid or evade the laws if they are so minded. It is ultimately not the weaponry of the police but the attitude of the citizenry that keeps our society from running amok and our system from splintering. It is doubtful that the presence of more statutes on the books would alone have prevented the already-illegal Watergate horrors.

After filing the Report of the Senate Watergate Committee which he chaired, a report which recommended dozens of new laws, Senator Sam Ervin added:

Candor compels the confession . . . that law alone will not suffice to prevent future Watergates. . . . Law is not self-executing. . . . It does not make men good. . . .

[T]he only sure antidote for future Watergates is an understanding of fundamental principles, and intellectual and moral integrity, in the men and women who achieve or are entrusted with governmental or political power.

In this country we are all, as citizens and voters, entrusted with governmental and political power. If Watergate spurs us all to understand better those fundamental principles and strive more diligently for that intellectual and moral integrity, then it can truly be a watershed for this country.

Then next time there will be watchmen in the night—all of us.

Sources and Notes

While drawing extensively upon my own files, books and recollections, I have also benefitted and borrowed from the wisdom and reportage of others. For the entire period in which the events under discussion took place, the *Washington Post*, the *New York Times* (including its Op Ed page), and *National Journal Reports* provided invaluable information and insights. The hearings, exhibits, staff memoranda, and reports of the Senate Watergate Committee, House Judiciary Committee, and Senate Special Committee on the Termination of the National Emergency, and the published Nixon transcripts (Bantam ed. 1974) have also been drawn upon throughout. Other basic reference works quoted or otherwise useful in several chapters, but like the above not individually cited, include:

Berger, Raoul, *Impeachment: The Constitutional Problems* (Harvard University Press, 1973).

Burns, James MacG., *Presidential Government* (Houghton Mifflin, 1973).

Corwin, E. S., *The President: Office and Powers* (New York University Press, 1940).

Dorsen, Norman, and Gillers, Stephen (eds.), *None of Your Business: Government Secrecy in America* (Viking, 1974).

Drew, Elizabeth, "A Reporter in Washington, D.C.," *New Yorker*, October 14, 21, 28, 1974.

Hughes, Emmet, *The Living Presidency* (Coward, McCann & Geoghegan, 1973).

National Academy of Public Administration, Panel Report, "Watergate: Its Implications for Responsible Government," March, 1974.

Roberts, Charles (ed.), *Has the President Too Much Power?* (Harper's Magazine Press, 1974).

Rossiter, Clinton, *The American Presidency* (Harcourt, Brace, 1960).

Schlesinger, Arthur M., Jr., *The Imperial Presidency* (Houghton Mifflin, 1973).

Tugswell, Rexford, and Cronin, Thomas (eds.), *The Presidency Reappraised* (Praeger, 1974).

My legal training compels me, however, to provide specific citations of judicial decisions, and to the notes that follow I have added sources other than the foregoing.

Chapter 1
1   *Newsweek*, Aug. 19, 1974, p. 15.

Chapter 2
1   Thomas Cronin, "Everybody Believes in Democracy Until He Gets to the White House: An Examination of White House-Departmental Relations," *Law & Contemporary Problems*, vol. 35, no. 3 (summer 1970), p. 573.
2   Thomas Eagleton, *War and Presidential Power* (Liveright, 1974), p. 220. See also the War Powers Resolution, 87 Stat. 555 (1973).

Chapter 3

1 John F. Kennedy, Foreword to Theodore C. Sorensen, *Decision-making in the White House* (Columbia University Press, 1963).

2 *Id.*

3 William Carey, "Presidential Staffing in the Sixties and Seventies," *Pub. Ad. Rev.*, vol. 29 (1969), p. 453.

4 376 U.S. 254 (1964); see also *Curtis Pub. Co.* v. *Butts*, 388 U.S. 130 (1967); but for suits by more private persons see *Gertz* v. *Welch, CCH Sup. Ct. Bul.*, B4177 (June 25, 1974).

5 In a penetrating article in the *New York Times Magazine* of November 10, 1974, Milton Gwirtzman notes that Congress's own budget has risen from $42 million to $328 million in the last 20 years while its staff rose from 4,500 to 16,000.

6 5 U.S. (1 Cranch) 137 (1803).

7 *Little* v. *Barreme*, 6 U.S. (2 Cranch) 170 (1804).

8 *U.S.* v. *Nixon*, 42 U.S.L.W. 5237 (U.S. 1974).

9 The Cherokee Indian case which gave rise to Jackson's alleged utterance involved no order against the President. *Worcester* v. *Georgia*, 31 U.S. (6 Pet.) 515 (1832).

10 For a summary of cases prior to 1957 holding presidential orders unconstitutional, see Glendon Schubert, *The Presidency in the Courts* (University of Minnesota Press, 1957), app. A.

11 *Youngstown Sheet & Tube Co.* v. *Sawyer*, 343 U.S. 579 (1952).

12 *Schechter Poultry Corp.* v. *U.S.*, 295 U.S. 495 (1935). It is questionable how applicable this case is today; see Ch. 7.

13 *The Orono*, 18 Fed. Cas. 830 (No. 10,585) (C. Ct. Mass. 1812).

14 *Jecker* v. *Montgomery*, 54 U.S. (13 How.) 498 (1851).

15 *Ex Parte Milligan*, 71 U.S. (4 Wall.) 2 (1866).

16 *Humphrey's Executor* v. *U.S.*, 295 U.S. 602 (1935).

17 *Cole* v. *Young*, 351 U.S. 536 (1956).

18 *Greene* v. *McElroy*, 360 U.S. 474 (1959).

19 *New York Times Co.* v. *U.S.*, 403 U.S. 713 (1971).

20 *Yoshiba International* v. *U.S.*, Customs Court, 1974.

21 *U.S.* v. *U.S. Dist. Court*, 407 U.S. 297 (1972). See also *U.S.* v. *Ehrlichman*, 376 F. Supp. 29 (D.D.C. 1974).

22 *Kennedy* v. *Sampson*, 364 F. Supp. 1075 (D.D.C. 1973), *aff'd* __ F.2d __,
Docket Nos. 73-2121, 73-2122 (D.C. Cir., filed August 14, 1974).

23 Some two dozen cases, exemplified by *State Highway Comm. of Mo.* v.
Volpe, 479 F.2d 1099 (1973); *National Council of Community Mental Health
Centers, Inc.* v. *Weinberger*, 361 F. Supp. 897 (D.D.C. 1973); *City of N.Y.* v.
Train, 494 F.2d 1033 (D.C. Cir. 1974), *cert. granted*, 91 S. Ct. 1991 (April 29,
1974).

24 *National Treasury Employees Union* v. *Nixon*, 492 F.2d 587 (D.C. Cir. 1974).

25 *Local 2677 et al.* v. *Phillips*, 358 F. Supp. 60 (D.D.C. 1973); but see also
Pennsylvania v. *Lynn*, 362 F. Supp. 1363 (D.D.C. 1973), *rev'd* __ F.2d __,
Docket No. 73-1835 (D.C. Cir., filed July 19, 1974).

26 *U.S.* v. *Nixon, supra.*

27 *U.S.* v. *Burr*, 25 Fed. Cas. 187 (No. 14,694d) (C.C.D. Va. 1807).

28 *U.S.* v. *Isaacs et al.*, 493 F.2d 1124, 1144 (7th Cir.), *cert. denied*, __ U.S. __
(1974).

29 It should be noted that Schubert, 17 years before the Nixon case,
argued that a President's ability to declare martial law, command federal
marshals and troops, and otherwise interfere in the judicial process made
him immune in fact if not in law from the reach of the judiciary. Schubert
(see *supra*, Note 10, this chapter), pp. 316, 323, 354.

Chapter 4

1 Hearings, Senate Judiciary Subcommittee on Separation of Powers,
April 10, 1973.

Chapter 5

1 *New York Times*, editorial, August 31, 1974.

2 See Thomas Cronin, "The Swelling of the Presidency and Its Impact on
Congress," Working Papers, House Select Committee on Committees, 93rd
Cong. (1973), p. 4.

3 See Arthur M. Schlesinger, Jr., "On the Presidential Succession," *Pol.
Sci. Q.*, vol. 89, no. 3 (fall 1974), p. 475.

Chapter 6

1 *In re Grand Jury Subpoena to Richard M. Nixon*, 360 F. Supp. 1, 9 (D.D.C.
1973) (emphasis added), quoting Justice Jackson's concurring opinion in

Youngstown Sheet & Tube Co., *supra*, 343 U.S. at 635. See also *Nixon* v. *Sirica*, 487 F.2d 700 (D.C. Cir. 1973). In effect, this affirmed Judge Sirica by dismissing Nixon's appeal and petition for mandamus. The action of Judge Sirica and the D.C. Court of Appeals was affirmed by the U.S. Supreme Court in *U.S.* v. *Nixon*, *supra*.

2   88 Stat. 297, 1974.

3   See *National Journal Reports*, vol. 6 (Sept. 7, 1974), p. 1344.

4   H.R. 12471, 93rd Cong., 1974.

5   41 U.S.C., sec. 11.

6   31 C.F.R. Part 515, eff. July 8, 1963.

7   *Youngstown Sheet & Tube Co. supra*, 343 U.S. at 654.

Chapter 7

1   *U.S.* v. *Nixon*, *supra*. Rehnquist, J. not sitting.

2   5 U.S. (1 Cranch) 137 (1803).

3   25 Fed. Cas. 187 (No. 14,694d) (C.C.D. Va. 1807).

4   71 U.S. (4 Wall.) 2 (1866).

5   67 U.S. (2 Black) 635 (1863). See also the Court's unwillingness to hear a similar court martial case in *Ex Parte Vallandigham*, 68 U.S. (1 Wall.) 243 (1864).

6   343 U.S. 579 (1952).

7   403 U.S. 713 (1971).

8   407 U.S. 297 (1972). And now the Court has ducked the issue again, *Ivanov* v. *U.S.*, *cert. denied, CCH U.S. Sup. Ct. Bul.*, B41 (October 15, 1974).

9   *U.S.* v. *Nixon*, *supra*.

10   Schubert (see *supra*, Note 10, Ch. 3).

11   *Durand* v. *Hollins*, 4 Blatchford's Cir. Ct. Repts. 451 (S.D.N.Y. 1860).

12   *In re Debs*, 158 U.S. 564 (1895).

13   *Wilson* v. *Shaw*, 204 U.S. 24 (1907).

14   *Isbrandtsen-Moller Co., Inc.* v. *U.S.*, 14 F. Supp. 407 (S.D.N.Y. 1936).

15   *Miss.* v. *Johnson*, 71 U.S. (4 Wall.) 475 (1866).

16   *Martin* v. *Mott*, 25 U.S. (12 Wheat.) 19 (1827).

17   *U.S.* v. *Belmont*, 301 U.S. 324 (1937); *U.S.* v. *Pink*, 315 U.S. 203 (1942).

18   *Maryland Casualty Co.* v. *U.S.*, 251 U.S. 342, 349 (1920).

19   *Ex Parte Garland*, 71 U.S. (4 Wall.) 333 (1866).

20   *In re Neagle*, 135 U.S. 1 (1890).

21   *Johnson* v. *Eisentrager*, 339 U.S. 763 (1950).

22   *Ex Parte Quirin*, 317 U.S. 1 (1942).

23   *Ludecke* v. *Watkins*, 335 U.S. 160 (1948).

24   *Chi. & So. Air Lines, Inc.* v. *Waterman Steamship Corp.*, 333 U.S. 103 (1948).

25   *Myers* v. *U.S.*, 272 U.S. 52 (1926).

26   *U.S.* v. *Curtiss-Wright Export Corp.*, 299 U.S. 304 (1936).

27   *Schechter Poultry Corp.* v. *U.S.*, *supra*; *Panama Refining Co.* v. *Ryan*, 293 U.S. 388 (1935).

28   See *NLRB* v. *Jones & Laughlin Steel Corp.*, 301 U.S. 1 (1937).

29   *Ludecke* v. *Watkins*, *supra*; *Fleming* v. *Mohawk Wrecking & Lumber Co.*, 331 U.S. 111 (1947); *Brooks* v. *Dewar*, 313 U.S. 354 (1941).

30   *Youngstown Sheet & Tube Co.*, *supra*, 343 U.S. at 654.

31   *Hirabayashi* v. *U.S.*, 320 U.S. 81 (1943); *Korematsu* v. *U.S.*, 323 U.S. 214 (1944); but see also *Ex Parte Endo*, 323 U.S. 283 (1944).

32   *Luftig* v. *McNamara*, 373 F.2d 664, 665 (D.C. Cir.), *cert. denied*, 387 U.S. 945 (1967). See *Mora* v. *McNamara*, 387 F.2d 862 (D.C. Cir. 1967). See also *U.S.* v. *Sisson*, 294 F. Supp. 511, 515 (D. Mass. 1968), and *Velvel* v. *Johnson*, 287 F. Supp. 846, 850, 853 (D. Kan. 1968), *aff'd sub nom Velvel* v. *Nixon*, 415 F.2d 236 (10th Cir. 1969), *cert. denied*, 396 U.S. 1042 (1970).

33   *Mass.* v. *Laird*, 451 F.2d 26 (1st Cir. 1971); *Orlando* v. *Laird*, 443 F.2d 1039 (2d Cir.), *cert. denied*, 404 U.S. 869 (1971); *Berk* v. *Laird*, 429 F.2d 302 (2d Cir. 1970); *DaCosta* v. *Laird*, 448 F.2d 1368 (2d Cir. 1971), *cert. denied* 405 U.S. 979 (1972); *Mitchell* v. *Laird*, 488 F.2d 611 (D.C. Cir.), *rehearing en banc denied*, 488 F.2d 616 (D.C. Cir. 1973).

34   *Holtzman* v. *Schlesinger*, 414 U.S. 1304, 1316, 1321 (1973). See also 484 F.2d 1307 (2d Cir. 1973).

35   *Ex Parte Milligan*, *supra*, 71 U.S. (4 Wall.) at 109 (emphasis in the original).

36   *Duncan* v. *Kahanamoku*, 327 U.S. 304 (1946).

37   *Woods* v. *Miller*, 333 U.S. 138, 146 (1948) (Jackson, J. concurring).

38   *DaCosta* v. *Laird*, 471 F.2d 1146, 1155 (2d Cir. 1973).

39   *Sterling* v. *Constantin*, 287 U.S. 378, 401 (1932) (emphasis added).

40   *Presidential Documents*, Ford, 1974, p. 1313.

41   *Pauling* v. *McNamara*, 331 F.2d 796, 799 (D.C. Cir. 1963), *cert. denied*, 377 U.S. 933 (1964).

42   *U.S.* v. *Porter*, 27 Fed. Cas. 599, 602 (No. 16,074a) (C. C. D.C. 1861). For an account of this and similar cases, see Schubert (Note 10, Ch. 3), pp. 323–324.

43   *Ex Parte Merryman*, 17 Fed. Cas. 144 (C. Ct. Md. 1861).

44   *Youngstown Sheet & Tube Co.*, *supra*, 343 U.S. at 596.

45   *Powell* v. *McCormack*, 395 U.S. 486 (1969).

46   *U.S.* v. *Barnett*, 7 Race Relations Law Reptr. 743 (1962). See also 330 F.2d 369 (5th Cir. 1963) and 376 U.S. 681 (1964).

47   See Schubert (Note 10, Ch. 3), app. A.

48   *U.S.* v. *Nixon, supra*.

49   See cases collected in Schubert (Note 10, Ch. 3), his ch. 11.

50   *Martin* v. *Mott, supra*, 25 U.S. (12 Wheat.) at 32.

51   *U.S.* v. *Burr, supra*, 25 Fed. Cas. at 190, 191.

52   Justice Jackson, concurring opinion in *Youngstown Sheet & Tube Co., supra*, 343 U.S. at 635.

53   *Baker* v. *Carr*, 369 U.S. 186, 217 (1962).

54   *Marbury* v. *Madison, supra*.

55   See *Holtzman* v. *Schlesinger, supra, Mitchell* v. *Laird, supra, Kennedy* v. *Sampson, supra, Mink* v. *Environmental Protection Agency*, 410 U.S. 73 (1973).

56   *Korematsu, supra*, 323 U.S. at 248 (Jackson, J. dissenting).

Chapter 8

1   See Arterton, June 1974 *Pol. Sci. Q.*

2   Schlesinger (See *supra*, Note 3, Ch. 5).

Acknowledgments

My views and information on the subject matter of the lectures upon which this book is based were sharpened through participation in several conferences or panels on the Presidency held in 1973–74. These included those sponsored by the National Academy of Public Administration (Airlie House, April 11–13, 1974), the Washington Journalism Center (Washington, October 15–18, 1973) and the Fund for New Priorities (Washington, October 4, 1973).

I am grateful to Mark Belnick for his invaluable legal research and to Burke Marshall, James MacGregor Burns, David Bell, Mark Alcott, Jeffrey Pressman, and Thomas C. Sorensen, among others, for their comments and criticisms on my initial manuscript. I am also indebted to Professor Burns for his willingness to contribute the foreword. All errors of fact and judgment, however, are strictly my own.

Frank Satlow of The MIT Press and John Crocker, Jr., of the Seminar on Technology and Culture at M.I.T. deserve whatever credit or blame is due for inducing me to undertake this project, and Marge Hornblower's long evenings and weekends of skilled secretarial assistance made it all possible.

Finally, for many reasons, including her patience, understanding, and encouragement during more vacation, late night, and weekend hours than I care to remember, my greatest debt is to my wife Gillian.

Index

Accessibility, of president, 153
Accountability, 83
  daily, 84
  increasing, 90
  judicial enforcement of, 134
  periodic, 83–84
  of presidency, xviii, 12, 56, 77, 95, 105, 153
Acheson, Dean, 120
Advisers, Nixon's, 155–156
  presidential, 100
Agencies, surveillance, 110, 111
Agnew, Spiro, 14, 51, 154
Aides, Nixon's, 158
Amendments, First, 39
  Fifth, 70
  Twenty-second, 27
American Revolution, 141
Apathy, of American public, 10
Appointees, Kennedy, 157
  Nixon, 93
  presidential, 98
Appropriations, 133
Armed Services Committee, 115
Army Engineers, 43
Articles of Impeachment, 50, 55, 56, 67
Attorney Generals, 136, 138
Attorneys, U.S., 136

Baker, Howard, 85
Balance, constitutional, 3
Bay of Pigs, 14, 18, 19, 80, 107, 141

Bazelon, David L., 127
Bernstein, Carl, 8
Biddle, Francis, 137
Bill of Rights, 49
Boorstein, Daniel, 67
Brandeis, Louis D., 108
Briefings, intelligence, 32
Bryan, William Jennings, 97
Buchanan, James, 28
Budget and Impoundment Control Act, 90
Bundy, McGeorge, 33, 92
Bureau of Reclamation, 43
Burns, James MacGregor, xiii
Burr, Aaron, 50, 119, 130
Byrd, Robert, 110

Cabinet, confirming the, 91–97
  early American, 96
  JFK's, 92
  "kitchen," 81
  members of, 34
Cambodia, bombing of, 59, 75, 124, 125
  invasion of, 20
  secret war in, 21, 86
Campaign, Nixon, 148, 155. *See also* Elections
Campaigning, "dirty trick," 15
Career service, 35 -37
Carey, William, 31
Central Intelligence Agency (CIA), 10

Central Intelligence Agency (continued)
  covert operations of, 111–112
  Ford on, 102
  Nixon's misuse of, 110
Charisma, 148
China, 59
Church, Frank, 115
Civil Service, 36
Clark, Ramsey, 137, 138
Clearance, security, 104
Cleveland, Grover, 122
COINTELPRO (Counter-Intelligence Program), 112
Cold war, 103
Cole, Kenneth, 100
Collaboration, 89
Colson, Charles, 10, 60, 139
Comity, 89, 132
Commager, Henry Steele, 4
Committee to Reelect the President (CREEP), 149
Committees, congressional, 45
Common Cause, 83
Communications, technology of, 8
Concealment, 107
Congress, access to information of, 104
  credibility of, 103
  Depression, 90
  Eightieth, 27
  and executive branch, 74, 79
  foreign hostilities and, 18
  legal service of, 133
  members of, 3, 22
  power of, 43, 86

and presidency, 9, 41–47, 87
  role of, 74
Connally, John, 14, 48
Constitution, Article VI of, 117
  framers of, 18, 51, 65, 85
Controls, wage and price, 59
Corwin, Edwin, 118
Courts, Congress and, 132
  and presidency, 47–52, 117, 131
Cover-ups, 6, 20
Cox, Archibald, 30, 62, 135
Credibility gap, 144
Crises, constitutional, 5, 27
  international, 71
  national, 75
Cronin, Thomas, 14
Cuban Assets Control Regulations, 114
Cuban missile crisis, 59, 76, 106

Dean, John, 13, 89
Debates, Kennedy-Nixon, 148–149
  legislative, 87
Debs, Eugene, 122
Decision-making, centralization of, 32, 35
  presidential, 31, 80
Declassification, 104, 108
Departments, of executive branch, 34
  heads of, 95
"Dirty tricks," use of, 15, 19
Disaffection, 22
Dole, Robert, 150
Domestic Council, Nixon's, 99
Douglas, William O., 68, 125

Eagleton, Tom, 21, 154
Economy, U.S., 4
Edwards, Don, 42
Ehrlichman, John, 54, 60, 93, 97, 100
Eisenhower, Dwight D., 29, 141
  on executive privilege, 18
  on Supreme Court, 128
Elections, congressional, 42
  financing for, 147
  local, 146
  1972, 10
Ellsberg, Daniel, 61, 120, 143
Emergency, 126
Ervin, Sam, 9, 60, 86, 138, 160
Ethics, public, 10
Executive branch, operation of, 35, 101. *See also* White House
Executive Office of the President (EOP), 100
Executive power, 46
Executive privilege, 18, 44
  claim of, 49
  courts and, 121
  House Judiciary Committee on, 69
  limits of, 50
  Nixon concept of, 54, 89
  Supreme Court on, 69
Ex Parte Merryman, 129
Ex Parte Milligan, 119, 126

Fairness Doctrine of FCC, 145
Federal Bureau of Investigation (FBI), 9
  and Capitol Hill, 43
  Nixon's misuse of, 110

Federal Communications Act, 148
Federal Communications Commission (FCC), 39
Federal Deposit Insurance Corporation, 35
Federal Reserve Board, 72
Federal Trade Commission, 147
Feed and Forage Act, 113–114
Financing, of elections, 147
Firepower, technology of, 8
Forces, commitment of, 18
Ford, Gerald, 13, 30
  on civil rights, 94
  on presidential power, 88
  public image of, 4
  veto by, 108
  and war on inflation, 31
Foreign affairs, 32, 85
Forest Service, 43
Framers, of Constitution, 18, 51, 65, 85
Frankfurter, Felix, 130
Fraser, Donald, 46
Freedom of Information Act, 102, 108, 127
Fulbright, J. William, 71
Fund, President's discretionary White House, 9
Fund, White House Special Projects, 76
Fund for New Priorities, 161

Gardner, John, 83
Garrison, Jim, 135
Gessell, Gerhard A., 10, 55
Great Depression, 71

Goldwater, Barry, 58
Government, open, 103, 105, 107
Grant, Ulysses S., 7, 63, 91
Grant Administration, 15
Grayson, C. Jackson, 32
Gulf of Tonkin Resolution, 86, 115, 124

Haig, Alexander, 30
Halberstam, David, 40
Haldeman, H. R., 60, 156
Harding, Ken, 42
Harding Administration, 15
Hickel, Walter, 20, 93
Holtzman, Elizabeth, 124
Hoover, Herbert, 89, 142
Hoover, J. Edgar, 56, 61, 110, 111, 112, 135
Hopkins, Harry, 92, 96
House, Col., 92
Hughes, Emmet, xv, 118
Hull, Cordell, 92, 96
Humphrey, Hubert, 46, 62
Huston Plan, 56, 61, 75

Ickes, Harold, 58
Impeachment, 7, 55, 133
  Articles of, 50, 55, 56, 67
  proceedings of, 66–67
Indochina, U.S. military involvement in, 59
Indochina War, funding of, 113
  legality of, 124
Information, access to, 31
  securing, 102–109
  White House and, 36

Internal Revenue Service (IRS), 10
  Nixon's misuse of, 15, 110
  White House and, 111
Isolation, presidential, 20, 58

Jackson, Andrew, 44, 48
Jackson, Robert, 116, 123, 126, 138
Javits, Jacob, 86
Jaworski, Leon, 50, 135
Jefferson, Thomas, 83, 140
Johnson, Andrew, 7, 63, 68
Johnson, Lyndon, 27, 29, 45, 141
  on civil servants, 36
  and Congress, 45
  national security and, 17
  and public opinion, 147
  war on poverty of, 31
Joint Committee on Atomic Energy, 45
Judiciary, federal, 10
Judiciary Committee, House, 8, 9, 21, 50, 53
  on executive privilege, 55
  on Nixon pardon, 79
  recommendation of, 66
  report of, 83
  Republicans on, 67
  and war in Cambodia, 86
Judiciary Committee, Senate, and Elliot Richardson, 94
Justice, Dept. of, 10, 134–138

Kennedy, John, 29, 92
  Executive Order of, 75
  and national security, 17
  Nixon and, 15

view of presidency of, 52
Kerner, Otto, 51
Khrushchev, Nikita, 106
King, Martin Luther, Jr., 17, 120
Kissinger, Henry, 58, 95, 97
Klein, Herb, 60, 155
Kleindienst, Richard, 54, 93
Krough, Egil, 143

Laird, Melvin, 93
Lansing, Robert, 92
Leader, congressional, 87
  heroic type of, xi
  Nixon as, 57
  strong, 59
Leak, 37, 38. *See also* News
Legislative branch, 41
Liaison staff, legislative, 44
Lincoln, Abraham, 29, 142
  courts and, 119, 129
Lobbyists, 156

MacArthur, Douglas, 76
Macmillan, Harold, 73
Magruder, Jeb, 61
Malek, Fred, 35
Mann, James, 12
Manning, Henry, 157
Mansfield, Mike, 77
Marbury v. *Madison*, 47, 49, 117, 119
Mardian, Robert, 137
Marshall, Charles Burton, 33
Marshall, John, 47, 49, 50, 88–89,
  119
Marshals, U.S., 136
Mathias, Charles, 115

McCarthy, Eugene, 40
McCarthy, Joseph, 18, 135
Media, president and, 144–147, 153.
  See also News; Press
Mideast conflict of October 1973, 58
Milk producers, 148
Mitchell, John, 137
Mondale, Walter, 83, 94
Moore, Richard, 63
Moynihan, Daniel P., 57
Myrdal, Gunnar, 10

National Academy of Public Ad-
  ministration, 83, 161
National security, 143
  Congress and, 103, 116
  definition of, 17
  Nixon on, 54
  presidentially imposed secrecy and,
    21
National Security Council, 58
Neustadt, Richard, 33
New Deal, 123
News, broadcast, 9
  presidents and, 16
  role of, 146. *See also* Press
New York Times, 56
New York Times Co. v. *Sullivan*, 39
New York Times v. *U.S.*, 120, 128
Nixon, Richard M., 29, 58, 128
  cabinet of, 92
  campaign staff of, 155
  and Congress, 45
  departure of, 3
  erratic behavior of, 6
  inner circle of, 97

Nixon, Richard M. (continued)
  nonimpeachable complaints
    against, 15
  pardon of, 5, 39, 66, 79, 89, 102,
    141
  on presidency, 89
  and public opinion, 147
Novak, Michael, 77, 142

Office of Economic Opportunity, 56
Office of Management and Budget
  (OMB), 100, 101
Office of Technological Assessment,
  47
Oil embargo, Middle East, 73
Ouster, Nixon, effect of, 65–70

Paranoia, 20
Park Service, 43
Parliamentary system, 79
Passport Office, 43
Patronage, 85
Pauling, Linus, 127
Peace movement, 20
Pentagon Papers, 56, 120
Personality, cult of, 144
Pierce, Franklin, 122
"Plumbers," White House, 19, 99
Political parties, 22, 149
Politicians, in Cabinet, 96–97
  and president, 137
Politics, reelection, 16
Porter, Herbert L., 129
Poverty, war on, 31

Power, congressional, 44, 45, 91
  control of, xii
  emergency, 113–116
  federal balance of, 132
  presidential, 8, 37, 43, 53, 72, 76–
    82, 122
  separated, 88
Presidency, and emergency powers,
  113
  imperial, 4, 83
  impotent, 60–76
  inherent limitations of, 29–33
  institutional limitations of, 33–52
  Nixon, 53, 54, 60, 61
  powers of, 28, 61 (see also Power)
  reassessing, 23
  role of, 12
  strong, 28
  Watergate's meaning for, 53
  weakening of, 63
President, access to, 156
  accountability of, 9 (see also Ac-
    countability)
  constitutional authority of, 29
  effectiveness of, 96
  leaks and, 38
  marketing of, 146–151
  measuring of, 151–160
  media and, 144–147
  mystique of, 139–144
  people and, 139
  political operating style of, 152
  popularity of, 14
Press, 5, 8
  distrust of, 20
  Nixon and, 58

and presidential power, 37
role of, 146
Washington, 39
Press conferences, 153
avoidance of, 41
"Project Responsiveness," 16
Protest movements, 20
and LBJ, 17
Public, role of, 10

Rather, Dan, 9
Rayburn, Sam, 45
Rebozo, Bebe, 17
Reciprocity, 89
Reconstruction Finance Corpora-
tion, 90
Reforms, legislative, 90
Reporters, Washington, 40. *See also*
Press
Republican National Committee,
150
Resignation, presidential, 68
Reston, James, 4
Richardson, Elliot, 30, 94, 97, 137
Rockefeller, Nelson, on improper
gifts, 94
as vice president, 27
Rodino, Peter, 9, 65
Rogers, William, 93
Romney, George, 93
Roosevelt, Franklin, 27, 29, 75, 92,
122, 123, 128
and Democratic Party, 59
and emergency powers, 113
Roosevelt, Theodore, 111, 122
Rossiter, Clinton, 83, 118, 126

Ruckelshaus, William, 137
Rusk, Dean, 92
Russia, détente with, 59

Schlesinger, Arthur, xv, 4, 18, 83
Schubert, Glendon, 121
Seclusiveness, 57
Secrecy, 57
and presidency, 107
Secret Service, Nixon's misuse of,
110
Senate, Special Committee of, 9
Seniority system, 90–91
Sherman, John, 28
Shultz, George, 95
Silent majority, 20
Sirica, John, 8, 10, 55, 88
Sloan, Hugh, 17, 158
Smoot-Hawley tariff, 90
Special Prosecutor, 5, 134, 136
Staff, Nixon, 157
Statesmanship, 32
Steel seizure case, 119, 130
Stimson, Henry, 96
Story, Joseph, 130
Strauss, Lewis, 95
Subpoenas, House Judiciary Com-
mittee, 65
Supreme Court, 21, 40, 47
Nixon and, 57, 65
presidency and, 48, 121, 128
Sumner, Charles, 91
Surveillance, agencies of, 110, 111
overseeing, 109–113
technology of, 8
Sutherland, George, 123

Taft, William Howard, 36
Taney, Roger B., 129
Tapes, Nixon, 102
Tapes case, Nixon, 48, 88, 117, 118, 121
Television, 8, 147
ter Horst, Jerry, 97
Term, presidential, 77
Trading With the Enemy Act, 115
Transition Task Force, Ford, 101
Treaties, ratification of, 43
Truman, Harry, 29, 76, 90, 128
  and steel seizure, 120, 130
Tuchman, Barbara, 5, 81

U.S. v. *Burr*, 119, 130
U.S. v. *Nixon*, 48, 50, 117, 120
U.S. v. *U.S. District Court*, 120

Veto, presidential, 44, 108
Vietnam, and American society, 20
  Congress and, 18. *See also* Indochina War
Vice President, choosing of, 155
  President and, 153–154

Wallace, George, 137, 147
War, 126
War Powers Act, 21, 46, 86, 91
Warren, Earl, 128
Washington Journalism Center, 161
Washington Post, 56
Watergate, lesson of, 7
  Nixon's response to, 60
  Vietnam and, 21–22

Watergate Committee, Senate, 133, 138, 160
Weicker, Lowell, 137, 138
White House, Eisenhower, 7
  Kennedy, 36
  Nixon, 60, 155
  Truman, 7
White House Staff, functions of, 97–102
Wills, Frank, 8
Wilson, Woodrow, 63, 92, 114
Wiretaps, "national security," 125
Woodward, Bob, 8